T ill
My I -1918

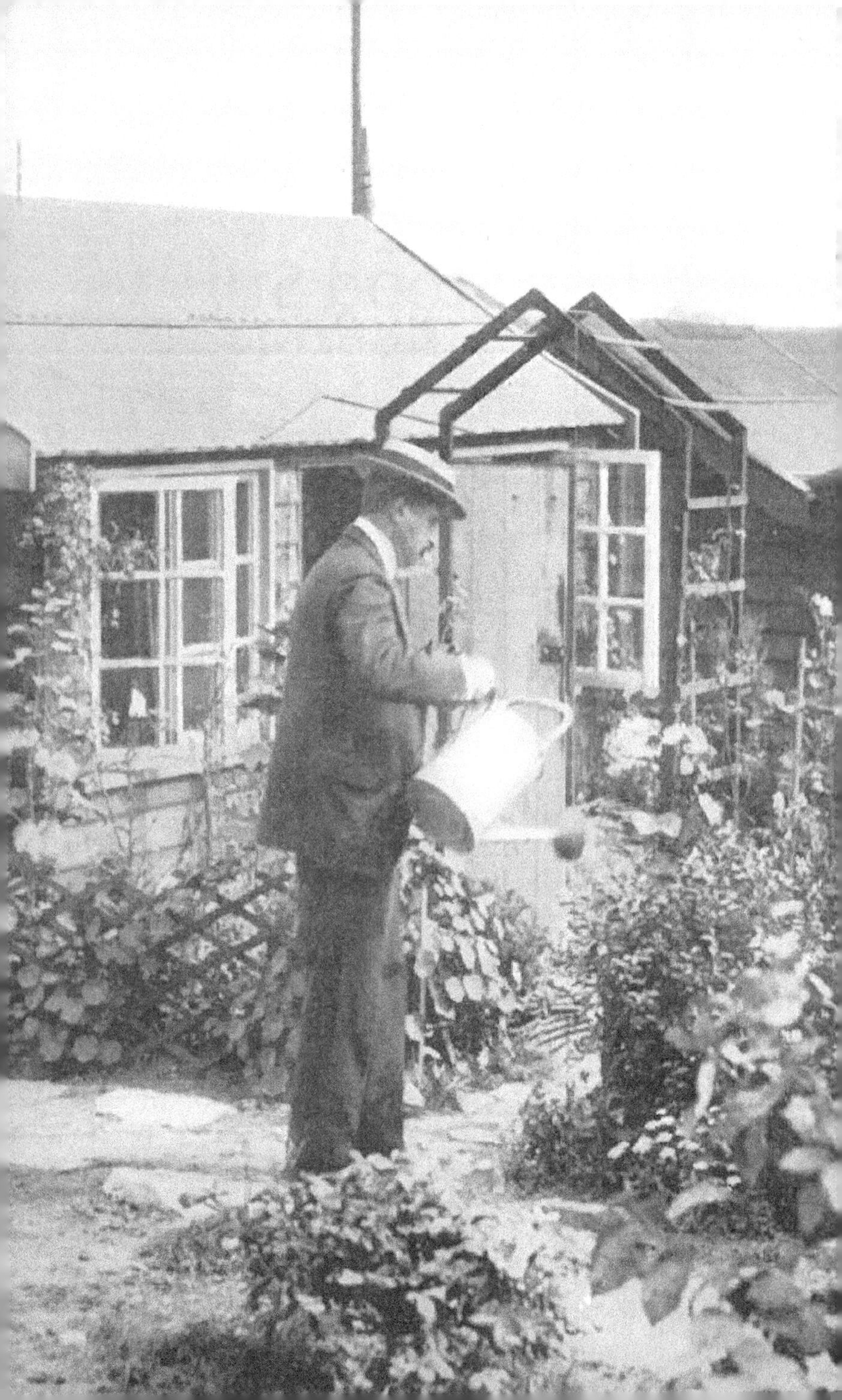

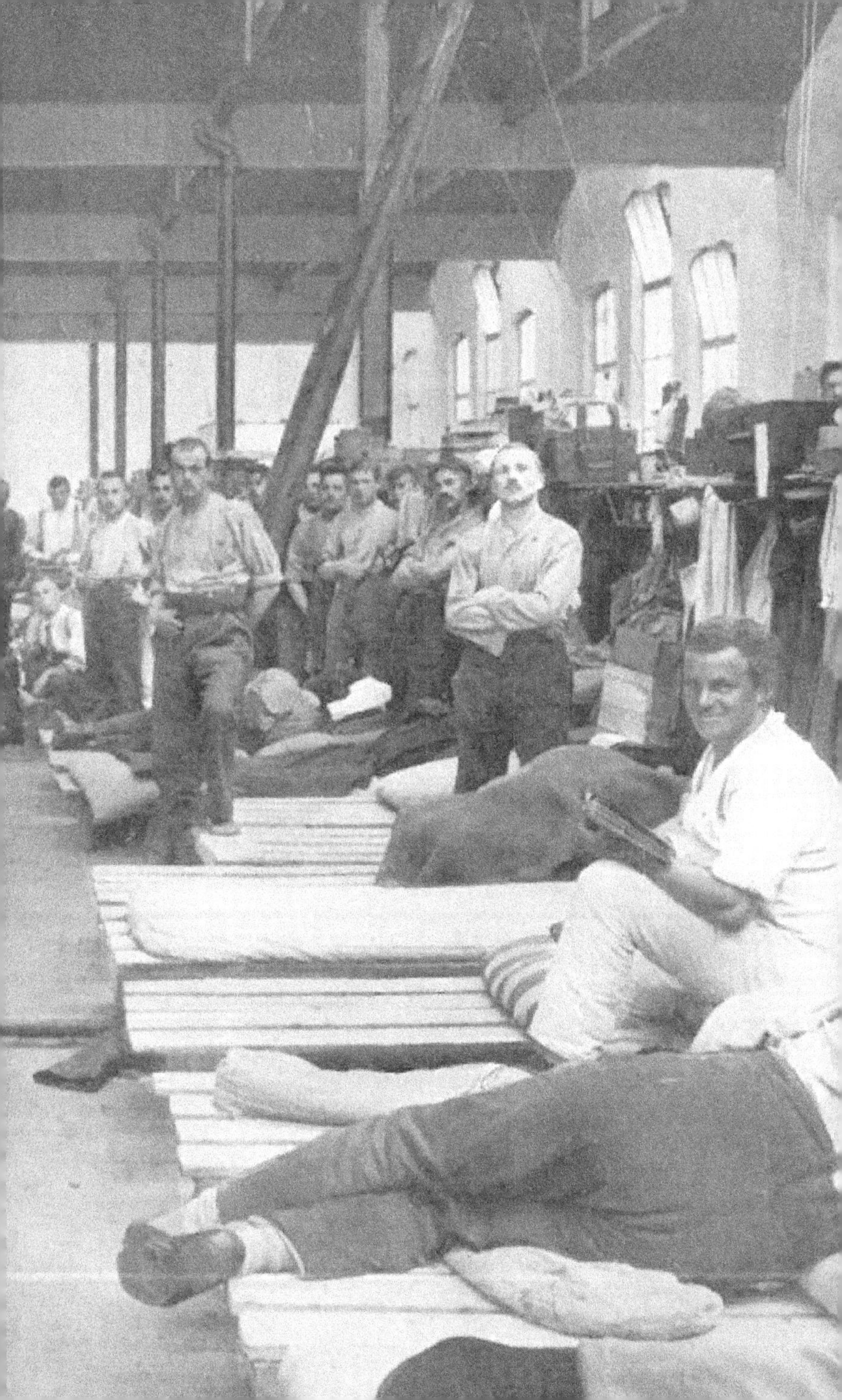

Time Stood Still
My Internment in England 1914-1918

Paul Cohen-Portheim

Introduction by Andrea Pitzer
Afterword by Panikos Panayi

RECOVERED BOOKS
BOILER HOUSE PRESS

Contents

3
Introduction
by Andrea Pitzer

9
Time Stood Still
My Internment in England 1914-1918
by Paul Cohen-Portheim

247
Afterword
by Panikos Panayi

Introduction
by Andrea Pitzer

The spell Paul Cohen-Portheim casts in *Time Stood Still* conjures a crucial voice from the past, that of a civilian detained in a British concentration camp during the First World War. How the Berlin-born Jewish painter ended up in detention is simple enough: he had the misfortune of being in England in August 1914 when Europe went up in flames. Unable to get a berth on a departing ship, he remained at England's mercy, until mercy, too, departed.

In an earlier war, Cohen-Portheim would likely have met a different fate. He might have sworn not to join the fight and been left at liberty. He might have been deported back to his native land. However, the expansion of universal conscription in prior decades meant most men of fighting age could be called up for service in 1914, making it easier to portray every German-born male in England, soldier or not, as a threat.

With his belongings in his apartment in Paris, his family in Austria and Germany, and £10 to his name, Cohen-Portheim was declared an enemy alien when Britain entered the war. *The Daily*

Mail beat the drum for mass arrests, and *Scottish Field* magazine asked, "Do Germans have souls?" Throw in the spy fever that had gripped England for years and the German U-boat that sank the civilian liner *Lusitania* in May 1915, and it is perhaps unsurprising that Cohen-Portheim found himself detained. A storm of technological innovations in the prior half-century (the patenting of barbed wire and mass production of automatic weapons) combined with anti-immigration legislation and the birth of modern propaganda to make locking up whole classes of noncombatants not just possible but a public spectacle.

Prior to 1914, nations had imposed what were already known as "concentration camps" — mass civilian detention without trial — in colonial settings. These camps were understood to be brutal. Cohen-Portheim mentions their use by the British in the Second Boer War as "a cruel expedient." More than a decade after that war, faced with detention himself, he hopes that "internment meant something quite different."

In his case, it did. World War I would transform mass civilian detention, spreading it to dozens of countries across the globe. Concentration camps moved into the capital cities of developed nations, into the heart of what modern thinkers liked to characterize as civilization. Hundreds of thousands of people around the world suffered the same fate during the course of the war.

Once Cohen-Portheim entered the camp system, the war destroying Europe and engulfing the world remained apparent to him, but always at a distance. He recognized that the sorrows plaguing detainees would be only a footnote to the larger disaster.

He also understood that he was luckier than many, and he lays out the details of his detention in understated ways that reveal both humor and heartbreak. The most powerful details from his captivity are often those which reveal his naïveté, particularly in the early days of confinement. Told that he must report to a camp the next morning, he follows the advice of an equally confused policeman, who tells him to "pack as if you were going for a holiday." Our hapless narrator brings white flannels and evening dress for daily life in a barracks.

Internment was not a holiday but a grim experiment. Cohen-Portheim measures the space allotted to each prisoner as six feet by four feet (twice as wide as a coffin, he notes). No amount of metaphorical bows put on the barbed wire — in the form of plays, correspondence courses, and libraries — could prevent the harm done by preemptive detention of indeterminate length. "Compared with life at the front," he writes, "life in a concentration camp was undramatic; there was no danger, there was no heroism, voluntary or forced. It was monotonous, it was drab, it was futile, and in that very futility lay its tragedy." Cohen-Portheim is unable to recall anyone untouched by mental illness after time spent in the camps.

Time Stood Still arrived in English translation in 1931, with *The New York Times* calling it "splendid" and comparing its power to that of Remarque's *All Quiet on the Western Front*. One of the key historical perspectives Cohen-Portheim provides is that the internment camps of the First World War were not monstrous merely to modern eyes in hindsight, once they could be seen as the bridge between colonial camps and the Holocaust. What today seems by comparison an almost idyllic kind of detention camp was, Cohen Portheim makes clear, evil from the beginning. His observation about the war — that it lay "absolutely beyond human imagination, that is why it could continue for years and why there is a danger of new wars" — is equally true of concentration camps.

After turning to contemplation of Asian and Chinese philosophy during his captivity, Cohen-Portheim remained a writer for the rest of his life. He rejected the reactionary nationalism of his day that made concentration camps possible, believing instead in an international community and refusing to blame the English for his internment.

His faith in humanity, however, waned. As his translator, Alan Harris, later wrote, "Cohen-Portheim changed some of his opinions in the after-war years... he became less hopeful about the early triumph of the spirit of Universalism, and turned his attention more and more away from the idea of going to school with the philosophers of Asia and towards that of saving a specifically European civilisation." By the early 1930s, Cohen-Portheim would argue in *England, The Unknown Isle* that the British Empire was the hope of humanity and "the champion of the world supremacy of the White Man."

Cohen-Portheim died in 1932. Had he lived a few years longer, he might have transcended this bigotry, if only because Nazi race theory would have directly targeted him. During the next war, as a Jewish man in Germany or Austria, or even Vichy-era France, events could easily have brought him into a death camp to face a more vicious fate.

In addition to bearing witness to a category of human suffering that was — and is — largely ignored, *Time Stood Still* endures as a prologue. During the First World War, concentration camps appeared to outsiders to have been cleansed of their colonial roots and transformed into a useful and humane bureaucratic tool. Yet by the time of Cohen-Portheim's death, they were (in Russia and elsewhere) well on their way to becoming charnel houses. Before the midpoint of the century, they would enter the pantheon of humanity's most horrific inventions. Here, however, he writes humanely about inhumanity, as only a detainee can, laying bare the concentration camp phenomenon in its early years and showing how even in its least lethal form, it was more than capable of breaking men's minds and wrecking countless lives.

Time Stood Still
My Internment in England, 1914-1918

by Paul Cohen-Portheim

This book was originally published in 1931. It is a historical text and for this reason no changes have been made to its use of language.

To Emily

Preface

There is a saying, attributed to Lord Beaconsfield, which contains a very profound truth: 'Most crimes in this world are committed through lack of imagination. If the murderer's imagination were vivid enough to make him picture the sensations of his victim there would be no murder.' The Great War was absolutely beyond human imagination, that is why it could continue for years and why there is a danger of new wars. People are genuinely shocked or grieved when one aeroplane smashes or when there is a pit disaster and a few human lives are destroyed, but when thousands of aeroplanes are shot down and hundreds of thousands of men blown up by mines the scale of horrors transcends imagination and people cease to care. That dulling influence of war on human sympathy is, I consider, its worst and most tragic effect. That is also why, in my opinion, there can never be enough books, plays, films, accounts of the war, never enough means of impressing imagination. That catastrophe was so gigantic and so complex that it can only be reconstructed by a vast number of single accounts of individual and limited experiences, and we are only at the beginning of such a reconstruction. Nor should these accounts be limited to those by people who took an active part in the fighting; one should know how all those countless millions we call the people lived — in France or Germany, England or Russia. The parents and the children, the old people whose declining years were saddened, the very young whose whole future was changed. Nothing is too small or ordinary, for all connects up, is part of the great fresco.

There is only one condition and that is strict truthfulness. When war broke out, leading men of all neutral nations were asked by the Paris newspaper, *Le Figaro*, to express their sentiments. Very few of the answers were in any way remarkable, but the great Danish critic and essayist, Georg Brandes,[1] wrote: 'The real tragedy of this war is that it has assassinated truth.' These were prophetic words. Truth was dead and propaganda had replaced it; that is why the task of this after-war period is to rediscover truth, not to replace pro-war propaganda by anti-war propaganda. This book tells of the experiences of a German civilian interned in England, and it is the author's aim to describe nothing except what he actually saw and experienced. It would be easy to write a lurid and sensational narrative if one were to transgress these limits and write of all one was told as facts, of all the horrors spread by rumour. That would most certainly heighten the narrative's dramatic effect, only it would, I consider, entirely destroy its value. Compared to life at the front, life in a concentration camp was undramatic; there was no danger, there was no heroism, voluntary or forced. It was monotonous, it was drab, it was futile, and in that very futility lay its tragedy. That existence was not dramatic like a *drame de cape*

---

1 A Danish critic. He wrote this in a public letter to the French politician and newspaper owner, Georges Clemenceau, in 1915.

et d'épée,[2] it had no trace of the romantic about it, it was a drama of the mind, like some of the Russian plays such as Chekov's, and its atmosphere was that of Dostoevsky's *House of the Dead*. Imprisonment is considered a severe punishment for criminals. Yet in this war hundreds of thousands of men were imprisoned in all civilized countries for no other crime than their nationality. I cannot see that any one country is more to blame than any other, nor how one could bear any grudge against that particular country or people which applied to one a treatment which the conscience of all peoples bore with the greatest equanimity. One has to be on guard against the danger of forgetting that what happened to oneself was but one of the very minor aspects of the tragedy of the war. It was quite a sideshow, I know, but I know that sideshow; it was one of many symptoms of universal hysteria, but a symptom as characteristic as any other, and the one I happen to have studied. As Corot the landscape-painter said of his art: '*Mon verre est petit, mais je bois dans* mon *verre.*'[3] There is yet another danger I had to guard against in writing this book, that of seeing the time of my internment in too rosy a light when looking back on it. One thing, I find that I have a better memory for pleasant things than for the unpleasant; furthermore, the period following my release was in many ways worse than that of my internment and made me feel sometimes I should have preferred it to continue. But the main reason is that while I condemn the system and think it has done untold harm, I cannot honestly say that it has harmed me. It was terrible sometimes, it held dismal weeks and months, but in its final effect I am inclined to bless it, not to curse it. That is, however, because mine is an exceptional case. In an epidemic which kills or disables most, there may be one or the other who, having recovered from the disease, feels better than

---

2 French: A drama of cape and sword.

3 French: My cup may be small, but I drink from *my* cup.

he did before. That, I think, is my case, or at any rate my way of looking at it, but this must not prevent me from considering the disease a disease nor induce my readers to think that I call good what in itself is evil.

Prologue

The weather was very lovely in Paris in the month of June 1914, and Parisians spent their night in open air places such as Lunapark and Magic City, amusement parks which were then at the height of their glory. Included amongst Parisians were, of course, people from every corner of the universe who had made Paris their home and who had long forgotten that they possessed any nationality except the Parisian. They formed a world of their own, a cosmopolitan society composed of Russian, Austrian, Spanish aristocrats, many South Americans and few North Americans, artists, writers, musicians of all nationalities and a good many stray French. There were even some English, though the majority of the English living in Paris formed a colony of their own. That curious world stretching from slightly soiled royalty to slightly camouflaged adventurers has been very well described in a book called *Trains de luxe*, by Abel Hermant, who was at that time brilliantly amusing and is now *de l'Académie française*. It was distinguished from afterwar cosmopolitan sets by the fact that it did not worship money and its possessors, but amusement. It had no prejudices and admitted anyone who was clever, good-looking, entertaining or in any way remarkable, but not people who were dull or vulgar and happened to be millionaires. Nor did it care for people because they had magnificent titles, little as most of those of magnificent titles would have cared to belong to it. It was vaguely aware of living on a volcano, but it hated to be reminded of its existence; it had in fact much of the charm which belongs to something about to pass, it was a new edition of the 18th century before the *Grande Révolution*. The catastrophe it sometimes apprehended would probably be due to similar revolutions, likely to begin in Russia and to spread all over the continent. It certainly did not apprehend a European war; that idea seemed absolutely preposterous to the people of this cosmopolitan and witty world of mine. If they had thought about it at all it would have appeared to them as incredible as a war of religion to the average *bourgeois*: such things were simply unthinkable in the twentieth century!

The Paris season was as good as ended and I was going over to England in a few days to paint in the country as had been my habit for a good many years. I would return to my Paris flat in October and visit my people in Germany and Austria at Christmas time. Meanwhile I had gone to spend the evening at Magic City, and one of the first people I met there was my friend, Count T. of Vienna. 'You've heard the news, I suppose?' he said. I replied that I had heard none. 'Franz Ferdinand has been assassinated by the Serbs at Sarajevo.' Franz Ferdinand was unpopular, his accession to the throne seemed none too desirable. A sad end, of course. 'What do you think is going to happen now?' I asked. 'Happen?' T. looked at me in sleepy surprise. 'Nothing. Why should anything happen?' True, things did not 'happen' in Austria. He added, however, as an afterthought: '*Le vieux crèvera de joie, peut-être.*'[1] *Le vieux* was

---

1 French: The old man will burst with happiness.

Franz Joseph. T.'s father held a very high position at Court, he was as intimate as anyone could be with the aged emperor — really: who should know if not T.? I worried no further about politics on that 28th of June.

Nor did they worry me the next few weeks in Devonshire where I was busy expressing red cliffs, seas, and sailing-boats in paint. The rival claims of impressionism, Cézanne, and cubism were very much nearer my heart than possible happenings in the Balkans. I read no newspapers. At the end of July I was going to stay with some friends near Richmond, later in the wilds of Surrey, and I considered the possibility of going to stay with a Greek friend in Athens in September, if the journey was not too expensive. I got to Richmond at the end of July and found everyone extremely worried. There would be war between Austria and Serbia and other powers might join in, though certainly not England. I thought I knew better, but decided all the same to pay a visit to my bank, the Dresdner Bank. There they assured me that all this talk of a European war was pure nonsense, and so I left my money with them. When I wanted it a very few days later they were no longer allowed to make payments, and I was left with about £10 until their regular business in London should be resumed. It has not been resumed yet. War was declared between Germany and Austria on one side, France and Russia on the other. The incredible was happening. I decided to go to the German Consulate. It was situated in Bedford Square, and there was a huge crowd outside it so that it was quite impossible to enter it. Some official appeared on the doorsteps and told the crowd to go home. They had chartered two ships to convey to Germany the military reservists; the others who had not served in the army should await events. The two ships were, by the way, held up by the British authorities and prevented from leaving. I went back to Richmond.

England did not declare war till August 4th. The suspense was almost intolerable, but in any case I had not the dimmest idea what I should do or what would happen to me. My flat and my belongings were in France, my relations in Austria and Germany, I myself with summer clothes, painting materials, and £10 in an England one could not leave. On August 4th England declared war; on August 5th an order was published from which I discovered that I was now an 'enemy alien.' As such I was required to register at the nearest police station. There they were frankly puzzled by me. My usual place of residence was Paris I said. 'But that is in France,' said they. 'The capital of that country,' I stated. So they sent me to Surbiton where finally someone inscribed my name and all sorts of particulars. I also had my passport stamped at the American Consulate, on the advice of some people I had spoken to while waiting in the queue at Surbiton — the first of very many queues I was to know. The Americans, being neutral, had taken over the handling of allied subjects in Germany and of Germans and Austrians in allied countries; later on they were replaced by the Swiss. There was a negro at the American Consulate one had to deal with and he was not a particularly polite or pleasant negro; this seemed to me rather symbolic of the suicidal tendencies of Europe at the time and has seemed very much more so since.

Up to that time a passport had always appeared to me a superfluous and rather absurd document. I had acquired one since once in Italy they had refused to let me have a registered letter without my producing one; but passports were things only Russians required when they travelled, as they were not allowed to leave or enter their country without one, a fact about which they were much chaffed by 'Europeans.' Well, apparently Europe was now obsolete, and passports really more essential than the people they belonged to. I was told of a dear old lady who came to the Russian Consulate and asked for a new passport, but when they looked at hers they found it was a German passport. 'Of course it is,' she said when this was pointed out to her, 'that is exactly why I want it changed. People are so nasty to me about it.' She was very disgusted when they refused to do so, and the Consul who told this story to some friends of mine regarded it as a great joke, but I really thought the idea most sensible. People were really, as she said, beginning to be 'nasty about it,' and the people they were nasty to were mostly quite helpless. On the second day of the war I read in the papers that an old waiter had committed suicide and, though this was a very minor incident indeed of the Great War, I have never been able to forget it. He had been employed at the Café Royal for countless years, but on the outbreak of war it was discovered, apparently to his own surprise, that he was German by birth. So he was dismissed, and turned on the gas, but he noted his impressions in a diary right to the end. The last few were: 'No more Napoleon stories now' (had one threatened his country with a new Napoleon?) — 'I feel very weak' — '2s. 3d. to the washerwoman' and 'I feel cold and I can no longer see the light.' Almost the last words of Goethe. Temporarily insane, no doubt — as suicides nearly always are supposed to be in England; I expect temporary insanity might also serve to explain the suicide of Europe which had just begun. One bought papers, papers, and more papers, hoping to see it had all been a mistake. Pessimists said the war would go on, might not end before Christmas, but that was, of course, absurd. Posters appeared stating that Lord Kitchener wanted 100,000 men and people were aghast at the figure, though it was perhaps better to be on the safe side. The streets seemed curiously dark at night and there were murmurs of a Zeppelin having approached London. I did not believe it; I had already begun disbelieving things I heard and still more things I read. I could not even bring myself to believe that people themselves believed what they wrote or repeated. Did they really believe that all the Germans in England, most of whom were ruined by the war, were spies? That every concrete floor was built to serve as a gun platform? The papers gave a vivid account of thousands of German soldiers lying heaped together, killed by a wonderful French gas called Turpinite after its inventor. That would, it appeared, soon end the war. Did they believe this, and did they not consider this invention an unspeakable abomination? There was no end of their credulity as it seemed, and the new invention appeared to please them. One read absolutely similar accounts from other countries, the symptoms seem to have been the same everywhere and they were repeated in exactly the same manner whenever a new country entered the war, down to 1917 and the U.S.A. On August 1st, 1914, mass hysteria had broken out — and it is latent even at the present time. Everybody felt something extraordinary was expected from him, but no one — except the soldiers — quite knew what to do in order to show his devoted patriotism. It was at that time the Government of Mr. Asquith issued that famous proclamation, that excellent advice: 'Business as usual.' To me at any rate the idea appealed very strongly, and I very much regretted being prevented from going about my business as usual; I had no longer any business, and landscape painting was hardly advisable under the circumstances.

At the end of August I was going to stay with friends of mine in Surrey who had very urgently repeated their pre-war invitation which I was only too glad to accept. I would like to say that my English friends were very kind to me as long as it was in their power to be so; there were exceptions, but they were formed by those of foreign extraction, German or otherwise, who felt none too sure of their own position, I suppose, and were fanatics as all recent converts are apt to be. I had to go to the police to inform them of my change of address, and that interview again was very remarkable. 'This is quite impossible,' they said, 'you cannot travel about, this is war.' I told them I could not go on staying indefinitely with my present hostess. She was anxious to get rid of me, I explained. This they were prepared to believe! 'Where is your registration card?' they proceeded. I told them I did not even know what a registration card was. It turned out that they had forgotten to give me one when I had visited them before, and incidentally that in the meantime I had broken every rule printed on it, in all innocence of heart. I don't know what would have happened to me if I had been caught transgressing and whether anyone would have believed my explanation. I was then informed I should have to have the permission of the Lord Lieutenant of the county; fortunately that was the very man with whom I was going to stay, which facilitated matters at once and seemed to reassure the police considerably.

At first it was delightful to be in a nice old country house and far removed from all war activities. My host was more than charming to me, both his son and his son-in-law were very intimate friends of mine and they were both present. Mr. D. regretted bitterly being deprived of his yearly visit to the Austrian Tyrol. His was one of the great families who have cousins and relatives in all countries and are therefore incapable of the prejudices of people whose family and experience are limited to their own country. Their greater knowledge and their international relations made the present situation all the more trying for them, however. They were in the same position as the Royal families, the higher aristocrats of all countries and the great Jewish families. I don't suppose that the Queen of Roumania, *née* Coburg, really loathed the Coburg King of Bulgaria or that the Rothschilds of Vienna wanted their Paris cousins destroyed by bombs, but even very highly placed persons had now to be very careful in what they did or said. Of all the liberties only that of thought remained — thus I was with people who could sympathize with my situation and feelings, as their own were in some ways similar. The country was lovely, the weather perfect, the people delightful.

And yet it was all very awkward. Again I had to be registered, as 'a lodger'; the village police thought they'd better have my thumbprint; we all pretended to think the proceedings a great joke, but we all felt uncomfortable and vaguely ashamed. We all showed a lot of tact, many subjects were avoided; in spite of all efforts there was an incessant strain. One evening I walked with Tommy, the son of the house, to some ponds amongst the heather. We stood still, looking at the reflections of the sunset clouds in the still water: 'Looks peaceful enough here,' said Tommy, and I nodded. 'I am going to enlist tomorrow,' he continued in a casual voice. I never knew a boy less like a soldier; he was small with a delicate face, he looked about seventeen; he loved art and artists and was studying architecture. A few months later he was an officer and a few weeks after that he was killed in Flanders. Nearly all the male servants had enlisted; then my other friend, Tommy's brother-in-law, also enlisted, though his young wife tried to keep him. He was a poet, a rather brooding and dissatisfied man, but of singular charm. He wrote in one of the advanced reviews even when already an officer; I remember reading his reflections while inspecting his men's rifles, briefly they were: 'I can't think why they don't shoot me.' He was killed very shortly after Tommy — by the legitimate enemy, however. It was quite impossible to stay on there. They said they wanted me to and made me promise to come back very soon. I promised and knew I never would and knew that they also knew. There was nowhere for me to go to except London. I had arranged a loan with friends by that time so that I could afford to live there, but I dreaded the solitude.

Where should I stay? Where could I stay? I went to a hotel I had stayed at before and found them willing to take me in. I would look for rooms later, as the hotel was too expensive for me really. I had to register, and they asked many questions. I felt worried and full of unrest; we were in November; the end did not seem in sight, it might go on till even after Christmas; how could I last out? How did people live through a war if they were in my situation? There was a lot in the papers about the internment of enemy aliens. At the very beginning of the war I had read that they had interned all those they considered suspicious characters. Very intelligible. But I was not a suspicious character and did not feel one. What was internment? I remembered that for the first time in history concentration camps for civilians had come into being during the South African War and were considered a cruel expedient. But at present no doubt internment meant something quite different. The papers had never described what really took place, but they, or some of them, seemed very eager to see all Germans interned. After the battle of the Marne a speedy termination of the war had appeared probable, but now that hope had vanished. People were in an irritated mood, the spy-mania reappeared (as it seems to have done in all belligerent countries whenever things went wrong). The police had been very anxious to know if I had no financial difficulties, a friend of mine explained this to me; they were interning all enemy aliens who had no means of subsistence, and as nearly all those who worked for their living had meanwhile been dismissed, that meant a gradual round-up. I tried to get permission to go to America as I heard that had been granted to some people, but failed to obtain it; that had, it appeared, been stopped. I began to look for rooms and took rather a perverse joy in stating my nationality on these occasions. Not one person objected, as I discovered, and it was interesting to see how calm and sensible the people were as compared to the ravings of the journalists. I took some rooms in a Bloomsbury square, and there I passed some of the most unhappy months of my life. Once more registration, and now one was definitely treated as a suspect, humiliating questions were put, references demanded, statements doubted. I had ceased to see people, my friends were in the army, some families already in mourning; they could not really want to see me even if they were polite enough to say so. The streets were pitch dark after nightfall, though at that time they tried the experiment of suddenly lighting up a number of streets in varying quarters by way of misleading the Zeppelins if they should come. But those evenings of exceptional brilliancy could hardly be called cheerful occasions either. The Zeppelins did come, the public got incensed, the papers fanned the agitation, the first deeds of violence against people or shops German or supposedly so took place. Life had become intolerable, I could not work, I had nowhere to go and nothing to go out for, I had been insulted in the street both as a foreigner (once) and for not being in the army (more than once), I could not sleep, I had had no news from my people since the war began, I was really 'worried to death.' I did not die, but I had a nervous breakdown, I saw a doctor and he ordered me to a nursing home.

I was comparatively happy at that home, at any rate, calmer. I had but one wish, to see nobody, and that could be satisfied there. For months I hardly left the house, and I got much better. And then something strange and unexpected happened and I found myself suddenly back in the world and with work on hand. A Russian friend came and asked me if I would care to design the costumes for operas for which he was designing the scenery. I was overjoyed if rather nervous: I had never done stage work before, and what about the obstacle of my nationality? He took some sketches of mine; he explained all about me to the people, and they liked the sketches and were supremely uninterested in my extraction. So that was settled and I threw myself into my work with almost hysterical ardour — I had never before known what a supreme blessing work could be.

This was a rebirth, a new life, a new career, a new enthusiasm, and it meant an income at last. The operatic enterprise I now belonged to was a war-product. It was international, the director being a Russian singer, while the others were Belgian (refugees from the Brussels opera), French, Rumanian, English — anything. They had taken the London Opera House and they were most enthusiastic and all most anxious to make a success of this enterprise on which their livelihood depended. They lived only for and in the theatre; those who were not rehearsing were watching rehearsals; the war was a very secondary consideration to them. The first opera I designed for was *Lakmé*, to be sung in French. The scene is laid in India, but there are Englishmen and women in it. It is a very old-fashioned opera and modern European dress seemed absurd to me (it was really too far removed from 1914!), so I decided on crinolines and the dress of 1860. There was a large chorus to be provided with Indian garments and I decided on a glowing colour-scheme for the big market scene. Quite plain and simple materials, but shading from ultramarine via purple, deep crimson, scarlet, orange to golden-yellow. The cool colour of the European soldiers' white uniforms and the women's light dresses was to form an expressive contrast. An Indian orchestra had been engaged for the performance, under the leadership of Inayat Khan. He was a very handsome bearded oriental, poet and musician at that time, but later, as I was told, a religious 'saviour' with a large following of more or less hysterical women. He was certainly a good businessman, as I discovered when I went with him to an Indian warehouse in the City to buy the material for the Indian costumes. He and the owner of the place bargained for hours, possibly about the percentage due to the poet. He also showed me specimens of Indian art, the worst type of modern chromos[2] they seemed to me.

I started my work feverishly, but as soon as I got beyond the stage of design to that of execution my troubles began. Not with the firm which was making the costumes; that was represented by a good-natured, elderly man of the Jewish persuasion, who was so delighted with my work that he offered me a contract to design for his firm. Thus I might have become a permanent professional designer if fate had not decreed otherwise. It was the actors I now had to deal with, who not only did not in the least resemble my beautiful figurines, but who found fault with what they were to wear. The women were bad, the men worse and much vainer still.

---

2   Chromos is short for chromolithograph, a coloured print.

The women would not wear crinolines, but by adroit flattery they could be convinced that they looked too lovely in them, and there was one nice stout woman who thought it a great joke. Lakmé herself thought I had overdressed her and insisted on larger and better *décolletés*; the chorus ladies, on the other hand, refused to appear barefooted. Still they were more accessible to flattery (if not to reason) than the males. Lakmé's father, the priest, was an irate Belgian who insisted on wearing the costume he had always been used to. '*J'ai chanté ce rôle depuis trente ans*,'[3] he said grimly, and he threatened to resign if he was forced to abandon his pseudo-oriental drapery. As his appearance — he was short and stout — did not correspond to my vision I thought I had better give in. But I was firm about the uniform of Lakmé's lover, the young British officer. He was a Rumanian, handsome and, of course, a tenor. He had to wear white and a sun-helmet; he wished, however, to appear in a Highland kilt. He agreed to the white ducks after much persuasion, but a sun-helmet — no, never! It would catch his voice, he explained, and I said that in that case he could take it off when warbling. He did in the end wear it the first night, but later it vanished.

In spite of these difficulties I managed, however, to get my things ready in time, and the director approved of what had been done. But my troubles were by no means over. Any theatrical production is a complicated business; an opera is infinitely worse than a play; an opera improvised out of nothing is unimaginably terrific. The different leaders were forever disagreeing violently in all sorts of languages; director, conductors, choir leaders, sopranos and tenors and basses and baritones were constantly threatening to throw up their job; and everybody was making everybody else responsible for everything. This is, I imagine, quite a normal stage atmosphere, but it was new to me and I found it

---

3 French: I have sung this role for thirty years.

trying, though it certainly made me forget the war. When at one of the last rehearsals the stage was filled with my resplendently colourful crowd, subtly shaded from ultramarine to yellow the conductor upset everything: sopranos left, high sopranos centre, etc. 'Colour-scheme be damned,' he said, 'how do you expect me to conduct?' And that meant giving up my scheme which I refused to do or making the women change dresses and altering some of these, which was at last agreed to amongst many maledictions.

The great night came, *Lakmé* was a great success, and the costumes and scenery were much lauded in the papers. But I was not there to witness the performance, for on the previous night an order had appeared obliging enemy aliens to be in their homes after 9 p.m. That was the first warning of menace to my new-found security, it interfered with my work as rehearsals went on to all hours of the morning, the director said some uncomplimentary things about police and politics in general (always interfering with really important work), but he kept me on. At that time they were rehearsing *Mme Butterfly*, and after that came *Carmen* with my costumes. While working for *Carmen* I attended the *Butterfly* rehearsals and they were most interesting. That short-lived operatic enterprise which ended in a small financial disaster is long forgotten, but I certainly have never seen *Butterfly* as charmingly done before or after. The leading lady was a delightful little Japanese soprano, her singing was perfect and she was obviously the only actress who ever looked the part. Scenery and costumes were due to a Japanese painter and they were exquisitely simple and effective. He also advised the European singers who represented Japanese characters and I shall never forget how he taught the 'Prince' good manners. That prince visits Mme Butterfly, and when the actor came in in a very princely, that is haughty, manner to see this lady of doubtful calling the little Japanese painter shouted excitedly: 'No, no, no, not at all!' He rushed on to the stage and explained: 'In Japan people polite, great people very polite, very great people very, very, very polite!' and showed how the prince should approach the lady with a series of deep obeisances. I thought it a pity that his teaching was confined to the stage.

Meanwhile I was working on *Carmen* and working very hard. I love Spain and everything Spanish, and the trumpery fashion in which I had always seen *Carmen* staged made me wish to show how it really should be done. I think those designs were really good; I had set my heart on them, but I was never to see their execution. I was really living in Spain at that time and the actual circumstances did not seem too bad. I had received the visit of a Dutch lady who — with the permission of the authorities of three countries — had brought me both good news from my people and money; I had very exciting work, fairly well paid, and prospects of lots more work; spring had come, and really the war could not last much longer now — surely both sides would see reason. Things in May 1915 looked better than they had done since that terrible August 4th, as far as my personal fate went, at any rate.

And then came the *Lusitania* incident.[4] In a day the whole situation was changed. There was a frenzied outcry from all the cheap press for internment of all enemy aliens = enemies of humanity: there were riots and disorders, and a few days later Mr. Asquith announced amid great applause that the Government had decided 'to intern or segregate all enemy aliens for their own safety.' Mr. Asquith had once more managed to make the crowd clamour for a measure long decided on by the Government as he had done when conscription was ordered, for, as I learnt later, the large concentration camp for civilians — large enough to hold all enemy civilians when finished — was at that time in a very advanced state. Probably internment was to have gone on more gradually and in a more orderly manner, but it must have been decided on long before popular clamour appeared to bring it about.

---

4 The sinking of the US liner *Lusitania* by a German submarine on 7 May 1915.

That decision was announced on May 13th — it would be a 13th, of course! But was it such a disaster? Would it really affect me, and if it did, would that be worse than 'liberty' as it had now become? 'To be interned or segregated.' 'Segregated' meant no doubt that one would be sent to live in some specified district. That had, I knew, been done in France, where people had been sent to places in the south of the country. A friend of mine offered to inquire from 'the authorities' what my fate was likely to be, and brought the reassuring reply that at present, at any rate, nothing was likely to happen to me. That seemed hopeful, but I could not reconquer my peace of mind, and I was not sure whether it would not be better to be segregated somewhere in the depths of the country and have done with it. *Carmen* was shaping well; most of the designs had been delivered; I was working on the last few. I still possess them; the others were executed by some firm or other. I never saw them again and, needless to say, was never paid for them, but what I minded most was that I never saw what my *Carmen* looked like on the stage.

One evening, it was May 24th, I believe, a detective called on me: I was to appear at the police station at 10 o'clock next morning. 'Why?' I asked. 'To be interned,' he replied. I asked him whether he was sure there was no mistake and he showed me the written order. I had not the slightest idea of what internment meant. 'What shall I pack, what shall I take with me?' I asked him. He smiled amiably — he was very amiable throughout that interview — 'I would pack as if you were going for a holiday.' It was to be a protracted holiday....

I followed his good advice and as a result found myself with plenty of white flannels, bathing things, evening dress, etc., but without a towel or anything else most needed. Having finished my packing, I went to see the only intimate friend I had left, and she tried to calm me, was sure there had been some mistake, and promised to try to find out about it. She also accompanied me on the following morning in the taxi which unloaded my luggage at the police station. Then I said goodbye to her and to the world. A heavy gate closed behind me. I found myself in a large courtyard shut in by high brick walls, and full of men.

Time Stood Still

He who beholds in action inaction, and in inaction action is the man of understanding among mortals; he is the Rule, a doer of perfect action.

Bhagavad Gita

Chapter I
Stratford, London E., and a Journey

There were all sorts and conditions of men, old and young, shabby and well-dressed — mostly shabby, however. They walked about, shuffled about, sat hunched up in corners. Most of them seemed unknown to each other and eyed each other suspiciously, a few stood in groups and conversed in low tones. Nothing happened. Hours passed. More men entered the courtyard. I had seen pictures of just such scenes in the papers, they were called: 'More enemy aliens surrendering peacefully.' So this was peaceful surrender — but what was the next step? I thought I knew, for I had asked the detective who had called on me, where I was likely to be sent, and he had replied: 'Stratford, I expect.' Segregated at Stratford, and not allowed to leave Shakespeare's hometown, as the Americans in force there call it, till peace came along. Well, there were worse places, and there would now be no tourists. Perhaps it was a delicate attention to send the Germans there, as they had always professed so great an admiration for Shakespeare. They went on acting his plays in wartime, while in England they had banned Bach and Wagner — how incredibly silly it all was — but in Germany Italian music had vanished for the same reasons. My thoughts drifted to opera, at least I could go on with my work — could I though! I had forgotten where I was and that I had surrendered peacefully. But the whole thing was preposterous, it would probably last a few days only, and then the matter would have been cleared up by my friends and the government convinced that costume-designing for *Carmen* was of no danger to the realm.

One of a group of three men standing next to me addressed me in rather halting German. Would I care to share a taxi with them? They had been allowed to use a taxi, as a special favour. Of course a policeman was coming with them. I stared. A taxi, where to? To Stratford, I was told, and learned that our destination was not the Avon but the East End. It was a sad drive. I had been able to picture existence in the Stratford I knew, but what could it be like in that of the East End? It was nearly evening, we were hungry and had little to say to each other. All three men were in the City, I learned, two were elderly, all three had lived in England for a great many years. Chance acquaintances, if there ever were any; I little thought I should spend years in their company, but human nature is strange, and these first casually met strangers had already ceased to be the complete strangers all the others were. One had a feeling of — very feeble — mutual support, one did not feel utterly alone, and thus were formed groups of often quite incongruous individuals which became permanent.

The taxi stopped in a narrow, dirty lane. Gates again, another courtyard, a factory. No more police; soldiers and officers instead. The luggage was sorted out, soldiers started examining it. My sketch books amused them immensely. 'This will do me very nicely,' said one of them. I never saw my books again. An officer stood by watching the scene indifferently. Someone handed me a metal disc which bore a number, and said: 'Give it up at the second camp,' after which I entered the building as I had seen the others do before me. I was faced by a very large glass-roofed hall, with a good deal of its glass broken. The floor was tightly packed with beds or rather *paillasses*[1] lying on a kind of bedstead; there were crowds of men — I had not yet got used to calling them prisoners — standing about, sitting, or lying fully dressed on these couches. They seemed a vast multitude, and numbered, as I learnt later, about one thousand. This, I thought, was the first camp, and it was worse than anything I had imagined, but I was going on to the second where I was to give up my number. There was an exit at the far end of the hall which would no doubt lead to it. But it only led into a triangular courtyard surrounded by walls. A train was passing by on a viaduct, there was a nasty smell, due, I believe, to chemical works nearby, there were more men, but there was no second camp.

I had made a mistake as I discovered: my second camp would be the big internment camp in the Isle of Man where we were to be sent on the following morning. Stratford was being used as a clearing station, though the majority of the men were there permanently. I felt both relieved and terrified; relieved because I felt I should have gone mad in those surroundings, terrified because I was being taken far away from my friends who, I still believed, would manage to set me free in a day or two — and that would surely be more difficult once I had been removed without being able to communicate with them. We got some sort of soup with bits of meat swimming about in it, served in metal pots, after which we were assembled in the courtyard and officially informed that we were leaving for the Isle of Man at 6 a.m. It must have been about 8 p.m. then; what was one to do with oneself? I had been given a couch, my bags were lying on it, why not unpack? But where did one's things go — I asked a bundle of rags lying on

---

1 Straw-filled mattresses.

the next couch — much to his amusement. There was nowhere, he grinned, you just took out what you needed; personally he had long given up changing for the night, or the day either. 'If you leave anything lying about, it won't be there long,' he added with a wink. I half undressed, lay down in utter misery. I felt so helpless: was one really never to undress or wash or unpack; was one to sit or lie on a sack, or walk round a courtyard and be counted, and have verminous neighbours who would steal one's things lying next to one, and a broken glass roof (the Zeppelins had done that, said my neighbour) over one's head, and could one possibly live under such circumstances? The lights went out at ten, only a few but very bright lamps burned on; the air was thick, people were already beginning to snore, sleep seemed impossible. But no doubt the second camp would be better, it could certainly be no worse — but couldn't it? If this was possible, if this was 'internment or segregation for their own protection,' anything was possible. Perhaps they would have dungeons there or cells. It was revolting, it was inhuman. If Germans and Austrians were considered a danger — dropping that cant about wishing to protect them — one could send them to some out of the way district, to an island even, but what possible excuse had one for treating them in this manner, worse than criminals really. I was furious, and then I had to laugh at a funny sight. A man walked past quickly, holding together his scanty garments with one hand, the other raised to the sky. A few more followed. That was what you had to do if you wished to visit the lavatory. It was like early schooldays, it was too idiotic. I thought of the men who had been in the taxi with me, middle-aged stockbrokers or something of intense respectability, waving their arms in the air if they wished to.... Even this life had its funny side evidently, so why despair? And perhaps after all one would be free to roam about in the Isle of Man, and it was supposed to be a lovely place. It could not be for long, anyway. I had seen the Isle in the distance once when

I crossed to Ireland; I felt very seasick then, I felt rather seasick now, but one must not give way — I wondered if there was a special signal for that emergency as well! Perhaps part of the punishment in the Isle of Man was having Hall Caine[2] read aloud to one. Ghosts with outstretched arms continued to flit by; perhaps they went there just for a change. I felt sleepy; I felt for my watch, it was still there, and it was past midnight. How ghastly it all was — but more absurd yet than ghastly.

I felt almost cheerful while washing, as far as possible, next morning. That place, at any rate, was done with! It was a cruel place and it was still more ridiculous. That first impression of prison life has never left me; to me its dominant note has remained its incredible absurdity, its utter senselessness, the thoughtlessness to which its cruelty was due — in short the lack of imagination it revealed. The journey to the Isle of Man was to furnish a good many examples. Its beginning was terrible. We were marched through the streets to the station, flanked by soldiers with drawn bayonets. The population must have known this was due, for in spite of the early hour the streets were full of a hostile crowd. The memory of a recent Zeppelin raid was fresh with them; this must have appeared to them as a sort of revenge. They spat, they insulted, they jeered, they threw things. I had been so utterly unprepared for this that I could hardly believe it was happening. Perhaps it was happening to somebody else, or was it a nightmare? Only one face stood out from the crowd, horribly real, that of an old woman with wild wisps of white hair blowing about it. She grimaced furiously and shouted "Uns!', then she grinned and nodded and said in a lower tone and with a curious sort of satisfaction, as if

---

2 A popular English novelist of the time.

to herself: 'Biby killers!' Then again the furious "Uns,' the smug 'Biby killers!' Her voice seemed to follow me all the way. She was quite drunk. I don't know what the actual distance to the station may have been, it seemed many miles to me.

I was prepared for a transport in cattle trucks — a train composed of very comfortable corridor carriages drew up, with plenty of room for everyone, and a very good lunch served by quite civilian and civil waiters (there is a connection between these adjectives). Man is a strange and illogical animal at any time, but this quick change was enough to make one feel slightly hysterical. People became vociferously cheerful: this was really an excellent joke, a holiday excursion — much better run than most excursions — at the expense of the British Government! It would be followed by a stay at the seaside, board and lodging free. Not much to grumble at, what? Families, ruined businesses, all worries were forgotten for the time being. This was a school treat, for the great secret of masculine psychology is that all men of all ages act and behave like re-become schoolboys as soon as their individualities are merged in a crowd. It was a pleasant journey. The train glided slowly through undulating green country. I had not seen the country for nine months; it looked serene and peaceful and undisturbed by war from the carriage window. We avoided towns, we stopped at no stations, but sometimes for hours on some siding. We reached the sea in the afternoon and the train drew up beside a steamer.

A change once more. On board the steamer we had suddenly become too dangerous to be allowed to remain on deck. We were hurdled and locked away somewhere below, there was no air, semi-obscurity reigned, and one had to stand. Fortunately the sea was calm. My three friends and I were very glad to be able to reunite, we felt quite old chums by this time. With hardly an interest in common we remained together for years after that day. I had already learned my first lesson, the impossibility of a separate and individual existence under these new circumstances.

I had lost not only freedom but all possibility of privacy and of individual action. And I consider that the loss of freedom is the more bearable.

The sun was setting when we disembarked, and the scene was full of beauty. A curved bay with softly rounded hills rising all around it in the dusk; soft, warm air; a slight drizzle. A little, friendly-looking town. If only one could have taken one's leave, said politely: 'Hope we'll meet again some time,' and gone off to the nearest inn! But instead of that we were again 'formed in fours,' flanked by khaki figures, marched away. Not at once, though; we waited for hours, God knows why; it had become quite dark. But up on the hill there were what seemed to eyes used to the blackness of wartime London myriads of dazzling lights. They looked extremely cheerful, and they reminded me of Magic City and Paris. 'Nothing will happen,' my friend had said — he who was in the know. But a good deal had happened since that night; this Magic City was Knockaloe Internment Camp and I was not a human being called by a name but an interned civilian numbered nineteen thousand and something, as shown by a metal disc to be delivered 'in the second camp.' We were marching through the town, the inhabitants, thank God, showing no interest whatever in what had long become a daily sight to them. I don't know what they looked like, it was too dark to see them, and during my whole stay in the Isle of Man I never saw the face of a Manxman or Manxwoman, nor even of a cat — tailless or tailed. Some of the men began to sing, which is, I suppose, unavoidable when people are marching: the soldierly spirit. But their choice irritated me, they sang: *Muss I' denn, muss I' denn zum Städle hinaus, Städle hinaus, und Du mein Schatz bleibst hier,*[3] an old German Lied of soldiers leaving their town and their sweethearts in order to march to battle

---

3   A German folksong: *Must I, then, must I, then to the village, must I then, village must I then, And thou, my dear, stay here?*

and heroic deeds, at least to maneuvers — really a most inappropriate choice for that occasion. Number nineteen thousand and something asserted his individual freedom by not joining in the singing. The chains of light came nearer and nearer, the mirage faded. Barbed wire appeared, long, endlessly long stretches of barbed wire, five or six yards high. And faces and faces behind the wire, thousands of caged animals. They called out to us, and as in a nightmare they repeated the cries of the East End crowd: 'Huns! Baby killers! Have they caught you at last!' This was not meant unkindly, but the form of humour peculiar to prisoners was as yet unknown to me, also I was very, very weary. At last a gate opened in the barbed wire wall, we entered, one's feet sank deep into slippery clay. In front of us lay on the left free space, on the right tightly clustered wooden huts, the whole surrounded by tall barbed wire and arc lamps. This was called a compound; it held one thousand human animals. Five compounds formed a camp, and this was Camp II. There were five camps altogether, I believe. The gate closed behind us. This, then, was 'the second camp,' the disc had been delivered, there was nothing more to be done but wait for liberation — which already seemed much, much farther than twenty-four hours ago in Stratford — or else for the end of the Great War.

Chapter II
First Impressions of Knockaloe

First impressions are by no means always right but they are frequently decisive. My first impression of Stratford had been sickening; my first impression on seeing Knockaloe Camp in daylight was one of delighted surprise, brought about, no doubt, by the contrast with the scene that had met my eyes the previous morning. Stepping out of the hut I found radiant sunshine, marvellously pure and bracing air, and a panorama of turf-clad hills. That is how, in spite of all that was to follow, Knockaloe has remained in my mind, for I am what the French call a *type visuel*, which means that the look of a thing, place, or person matters most to me. When choosing a house or flat I have always been apt to consider the view from the window more important than more practical matters, and if I had to choose an internment camp — which I hope to God I shall never have to again — I should be guided by similar considerations. This is apt to annoy other people a good deal. Knockaloe was considered the most distasteful of all camps, the one where hardships were worst and conditions most unpleasant, that is why I feel apologetic to my fellow prisoners when I state that I rather liked being there. It is only fair, however, to add that my stay there was short and that we had marvellous summer weather. The case of the men who were there for years and of those who were transferred there towards the end of the war or even after the cessation of hostilities, after having got used to the superior comforts gradually achieved in other camps, is, of course, a very different one. In 1918 and 1919 Knockaloe apparently contained hordes of completely brutalized or broken men — I say apparently because I have not seen that Knockaloe, but only heard about it from people I am inclined to trust. Not that one can altogether trust any other man's word on such matters as war or prison experiences; facts are few; it is the atmosphere which is all-important and that affects different people in a different manner. Thence the quarrels about war novels, some affirming that a book gives the exact truth: 'That is just what the war was like,' others contradicting them violently. There were as many aspects of war as there were soldiers, as many aspects of life in an internment camp as there were interned.

There was certainly little to charm one in that 'compound' if one took no interest in the view. There were a dozen or more long, low wooden huts, each of which housed about forty men. When we arrived there our huts contained a long table and a heap of *paillasses* piled up in a corner, otherwise they were quite empty. Nothing was ready, everything but half-finished. Evidently the intention of the Government had been to finish the camp first and intern the people after, but they had given way to popular clamour, and now transports of prisoners were pouring daily into hastily erected camps which were not prepared for their reception. We had had some sort of a meal, standing up, the night of our arrival, and the only good thing about it had seemed to me the butter which looked clean and fresh. I had ventured to say so and thereby earned a reputation for great foolishness, for the butter was margarine, an article of diet I may have tasted before but had never seen. Nor have I ever become an expert in spite of many years' acquaintance with it. I was tired enough to sleep; my troubles began when I wanted to wash next morning. The wash-house was yet to arise; so far there were only buckets which could be put on the ground somewhere after having been filled at the pump. I had no towel with me (having packed for 'a holiday'), but I managed to borrow one. I found washing *en plein air* rather pleasant, though it took an acrobat to keep an already washed foot clean while washing the other. By the time the lavatory arrangements were complete I was rather sorry to have to wash indoors. Those buckets were most useful, they served for everything: water for washing, soup, and — well, everything. One tried to believe that they did not get mixed up.

The first morning was devoted to a most solemn ceremony. We were formed into a square to await the visit of the Commandant, overlord of all prisoners of all Knockaloe, who was coming to receive us into his realm. We waited what seemed a long time and then the great man appeared at last. He was or looked very old, rather peevish and at the same time rather shy. I believe he felt uncomfortable. All sorts of old colonels had been dug out of their retirement, and probably they did not choose the most eminent soldiers for jobs of that sort. On the other hand at that early period of the war the officers doing duty in the prisoners' camp were officers of the old army and very much preferable as a class to those who followed them later. This old man certainly was what one must — for want of a better or more intelligible term — describe as a gentleman, that is why he did not care for his job and did not enjoy this particular show. Also at that time he had to repeat that performance every other day, when a new lot of one thousand stared at him with hostility, fear, anger, or amusement, according to temperament, or more likely with a mixture of all these feelings.

He began his speech, that speech he had to make every other day, in a rather quavering but not unpleasant voice. What he said — or what I remember of his speech was: 'If you will obey my orders I will treat you with kindness and consideration'; this sounded good, but he continued, without interruption and in the same low, monotonous tone: 'Anybody attempting to escape will be warned once and then shot' — and that sounded neither considerate nor particularly kind to my civilian ears. The continuation was unexpected. He pointed vaguely to the hills and said in a raised voice: 'The latrines will be finished soon [pause] I hope.' And that was all, but his hope did not materialize for many days, and then it materialized in the opposite direction to the one he had indicated. Meantime there were buckets and *plein air* and though it may sound absurd this was felt as extremely humiliating and disgusting by most. In fact, one could not get used to it ever (even a good many animals seek privacy on these occasions), only I must add that there were also quite a number of men who not only did not mind this but actually invited each other to proceed to that act in groups.

After the Commandant had had his say a German interpreter repeated his words. He was far more impressive: a soldier born. He shouted at the top of his voice: '*Der Herr Kommandant hat gesagt*', etc. And that ended the ceremony. And now, what next? Now there was nothing to do, nothing at all, nothing whatsoever, nothing — for how long? There was a sort of shanty called a canteen, standing just outside the wire, with its counter open to the camp, where one might try to buy something. No matter what, one had nothing one needed, so everything would be welcome. Hundreds were waiting already; I waited for about two hours and everything had been sold out when my turn came.

My dream had been some string, some ink possibly. But if I had not achieved my object I had yet not waited in vain; I had learned a new word which was more than a word, quite an illumination in fact. That word was: *Schiebung*, and I think it was the most frequently used word in all prisoner camps. It is not to be found in any dictionary and I don't think it existed before the war. The verb *schieben* means 'to push', 'to shove', 'put a thing in some other place'; after 1914 it came to mean all fraudulent dealing, all pushing oneself into someone else's place; a *Schieber* became almost a recognized profession the more war restrictions made honest dealing impossible. And a *Schiebung* was every act by which you gained an illegitimate advantage, and in a prisoners' camp every advantage is illegitimate and everyone always suspected of trying to gain one. Some men there had shouted *Schiebung* perhaps because one man had tried to get in front of another, perhaps because someone had bought more than one bottle of ink (and might try to resell if there should be a shortage), perhaps simply as a joke. But that mentality was anything but a joke, it expressed all the envy, distrust, and hatred which that unnatural mode of life, that compulsory existence in common had already bred. From 1914 onward everyone in the belligerent countries lived under a system of coercion and it soon became apparent that it was not as difficult to coerce the peoples as some had feared and others hoped. All the Smiths were quite willing to do as they were told and to put up with all sorts of hardships or dangers. But on one condition only: all the Browns and all the Joneses must bear the same privations and face the same risks. Wherever there was preferential treatment accorded or achieved by push, there, hatred and malice arose, but this was intensified a thousand times in prisoners' camps, for two reasons. First, such a camp has no accepted hierarchy to start with, while civilian society has its class distinctions and the army its grades; secondly, there is nothing or next to nothing in such a life to turn away people's thoughts from the real or imaginary wrongs done to them. The original and primary wrong they resent is of course the fact of their imprisonment, the fact of being punished without having committed any crime, but they cannot go on thinking of this for years. Very soon hatred and suspicion turn against their enforced comrades in misfortune, for the contact with them is incessant and everlasting, presenting an endless variety of occasions for new friction, whereas they hardly come into contact and have no intercourse with their official 'enemies,' that is, the soldiers who guard the barbed wire and the officers who count their numbers twice a day.

I needn't say that this was by no means clear to me that first morning at Knockaloe. *Schiebung* had sounded vaguely ominous, but I soon forgot about it again. There was a slope covered with coarse grass where I went to lie down. The sky was blue overhead and the sun shone, why not take a sunbath? This was really rather pleasant, I thought, a sort of boy scout or Wild West existence, not to be altogether despised. One could well put up with it for a week — for it might be a week or perhaps even a little longer before I would be released.... Meanwhile I had a feeling of great rest, of calm after the storm, and I felt tired enough. The worst had happened. I could no longer be imprisoned, because I was imprisoned; I could only be released how. And the present state of affairs had great compensations! The more I reflected the more I thought that even a month here might not be so bad. I gave no thought to the people around me, they played no part in my life as yet. I thought of myself only. There was a feeling of security here, nothing could happen to one, it had all happened. There was nothing to hide from anyone: everyone else was in the same situation, there was not that unbearable strain of relations with one's surroundings. I discovered some very concise advantages I had never considered before: as a prisoner I should be allowed to correspond with my mother, I should at last get fairly regular news of all the people I was fond of over there, I should also be able to have money sent from abroad. Then, well, after a month or so I would be released, autumn would be near then and must surely mean the end of the war. Another winter was quite unthinkable.

In the afternoon I changed into what seemed to me clothes appropriate to the surroundings, white flannels. This amused a number of people exceedingly, and I was asked whether I intended to go on in that manner. I replied that I had every intention of doing so, which amused them more than ever. And yet it was a very wise move though quite an unconsidered one. I can imagine no circumstances where it is more necessary to stick strictly to the outward decencies and conventions of life. They cease to be taken for granted, they become an effort, but also they become a symbol of resistance to outward circumstances; they come to mean that one will not give in, that one remains oneself in no matter what company or place, they become a strong and most necessary moral support. One need not dress there, one need not shave every day or at all, one need not wash — in fact, there was absolutely nothing one need do except rise and retire at fixed hours and stand still to be counted. Otherwise you can let yourself go to any extent and in any way you like. That is exactly why one must create one's own duties and obligations, and one's inner conduct and outer appearance are inevitably interdependent; self-respect and shaving brush live in mystical union.

Our luggage was distributed to us that afternoon, one of my two trunks had disappeared and it never turned up again. But there was quite enough left to embarrass me terribly, and no possibility of unpacking a thing. I had a great piece of good luck the next day, however, for I managed to get hold of two nails. Very few acquisitions in my life have given me greater satisfaction: one could hang up a few garments now, it was a beginning of a return to normality. The next day I was enriched by two small boards which a man sold to me. This was the beginning of *Schiebung*, of course, for no such things as nails or boards were to be bought legitimately, they could only be smuggled into camp with the help of outside agencies, and that help had obviously been paid for. These two slanting boards formed a headrest, and sleep became more possible. Matters were improving. I rearranged the contents of my trunk, putting the more necessary things on top. But the trunk left to me did not contain many necessities; on the other hand, it was full of all the paraphernalia of evening dress.

Chapter III
Organization of Knockaloe

I do not know how it came about, but all at once the camp seemed to have become a sort of organized community. In the first days it had been a rabble, or rather two rabbles, for when our rabble arrived the camp was already half filled with a previous batch of prisoners. The two batches were very unlike. Ours consisted mostly of men who had lived for years, in some cases nearly all their lives, in England: businessmen, merchants, well-to-do people, but also waiters, hairdressers, small tradesmen. A middle-class collection of many shades. Our predecessors were entirely different. They were people who had been taken off steamers and cargoes, German or others. They were mostly sailors, but there were a good many nondescript and some rather romantic individuals amongst the lot. I don't know the reason of this incongruous mixture. It was rather exceptional, for the authorities tried as a rule to keep the classes separate. There was a perfect example of that policy in one of the compounds of Knockaloe which was inhabited solely by men whom the French papers invariably allude to as *'tristes individus'* or as *'peu intéressants,'* which means that they live on the earnings of women more poetically called *'filles denjoie.'* There had been, I learnt, a flourishing trade in that article of export from Hamburg to London, and the *tristes individus* had followed the daughters of joy in order to keep an eye on them. The neighbourhood of Tottenham Court Road had been their gathering place, but at the outbreak of war the men had been interned and later on sent to Knockaloe. The women were, I suppose, sent out of the country, but the fate of the men seemed more extraordinary, for surely of all prisoners they were the least capable of carrying on in an internment camp. What could one thousand *tristes individus* do with not one daughter of joy between them, I wondered, and had there really been exactly one thousand of them to fill one of those neat compound cages or, if there were more, had they overflowed into other and more virtuous cages; if there were less, had there been padding? Or was the whole tale a myth — there was no way of finding out the truth, for one did not come into contact with inmates of other compounds, except of the two adjoining one's own to whom one could shout through the wire.

Our compound, at any rate, was mixed, and perhaps that made some sort of interior administration all the more necessary, but all the same, I wonder how it created itself out of nothing. There was a 'captain' to every hut, and a 'chief-captain' to head them all, and they must have been elected, but why one should have voted for anyone in particular out of that crowd of unknown people I cannot imagine. I suppose I didn't vote, and I was certainly surprised when I discovered our hut had a captain who looked like one of the stout, middle-aged gentlemen in frock coats who said 'Anything I can do for you, sir?' to one in London's great emporiums. He quite felt the importance of his position though; he really looked on himself as a superior officer, and the strange part was that there were a good many people who shared his opinion and who liked having a person of authority above them! I don't know whether that state of things belongs to all prison life and whether hard labour men elect a chief who is majestically condescending to them, but humble and servile to the jailers.

Things shaped themselves gradually. True, the 'latrines' were still far from finished, but chairs had arrived, and one now sat down to meals, which seemed as odd at first as washing within walls when the washhouse was completed, and it had suddenly become immoral and a serious offence to wash out of doors. The showers were a great boon though, and I took much pride in having a shower bath without allowing the water to extinguish my cigarette. The canteen was open for longer hours now, and one could buy chocolates and apples there, but the food remained awful and insufficient, nor was being assured that we were treated exactly the same as British prisoners were being treated in Germany much of a consolation. There was watery soup with bits of grease swimming about in it, or else some stringy lumps of meat, and the fresh air made one feel very hungry, so there was plenty of grumbling.

About that time I heard from London that it was very difficult to do anything for one once one had actually been interned, but still there was a chance, and no need to despair. That did not trouble me so very much, for I was just beginning to enjoy the advantages of my new status. I had got my first letters from home and my people had got mine. One was allowed to write twice a week, on one page of glazed paper, and it was forbidden to mention either the war or conditions in camp. Of course all letters had to pass a censor. That left really nothing to write about, as one no longer knew anything outside the camp, but it served at least as a sign of life. We were now in the summer of 1915, the war was a year old, and I had only heard once from home until then. Money arrived; it had to be addressed to the Camp Bank which took care of it and allowed one to draw £1 a week. That was a great personal relief, but it instantly introduced 'social injustice' and class distinction into what would otherwise have become a communist society. This men-state now had two sharply divided classes, the £1 a week class and the moneyless class, the capitalist and the proletarian. I don't know what the proportion may have been in the other compounds, in ours the capitalists hardly amounted to 10 percent. Nearly 50 percent of the inmates were sailors; of the other 50 roughly 40 had been waiters, barbers, small tradesmen, or servants. The remaining 10, the capitalist class, was composed of businessmen or young clerks. There was no one over 50 (for men above military age were repatriated on both sides), there was no one under 18 years of age; it was a society without women, without children, and without old people. Ninety percent of the men had no income now they were interned; it stands to reason that they made every effort to make money, it will also be understood that there were but few possibilities of doing so. Commerce, they say, obeys the law of supply and demand; I have certainly never seen such an overwhelming amount of supply and such an infinitely restricted demand! There were at least one hundred men or youths anxious to clean your shoes, and never in my life have my shoes looked so brilliant and been cleaned so many times a day, though the circumstances really did not call for it. We had over eighty barbers, but I could do no more for them than be shaved once a day, which sufficed, however, to make me highly popular with them. Their charge — see supply and demand — was one penny, but they did not object to the degradation of a tip of a halfpenny or more. And really both shoe-blacks and barbers were quite superfluous, for every hut had half a dozen 'stewards' to do the waiting and cleaning who were only too anxious to make a little extra money, and if you were known as one of the plutocrats — which you inevitably were — you simply had to accept the offers of one of the many who wished to become your 'private valet' — Noblesse oblige! True, such a post was rather a desirable one, for there was no work to do: no cleaning and sweeping, no errands, no clothes to press or silver to clean. A pity really, for my own valet would have done all that and a good deal more most perfectly. He was a very grand person indeed, and his last post but one had been that of valet to the Khedive. His name was Charlie, he was about forty, and always in the best of tempers; a very charming man really who would have made a perfect butler in the most baronial of halls. After leaving the Egyptian monarch he had been steward on a big liner, and that was how he came to be at Knockaloe. It was Charlie who cleaned my shoes for the very first time every morning, also he rolled up my *paillasse* and folded my cover. That is all he ever did as far as I remember, but the salary he received corresponded to the extent of his efforts. One could also by payment find a man who would replace you at your weekly turn of potato peeling. I tried that work once, but my conception was considered too cubist. All things considered, the social problem had found a fairly satisfactory solution during these first weeks in the Isle of Man.

On the day of my arrival I had been urged by my taxi-friends to subscribe a petition to be removed to the internment camp at Wakefield. Wakefield was a paradise compared to this, they said, it was one of the two 'gentlemen's camps' the Government had created (the other being at Douglas, Isle of Man) and much the better of the two. Its inmates had great privileges and relative liberty. I had put my name on the list and then I had forgotten about it. After all I might yet be released — that is how I had come to think of that chance — and, meanwhile, I did not dislike my life here. The camp was, in its way, a curious and interesting place once one had got used to its obvious drawbacks. I have always been interested in human beings and here there were a great many types I should never have come in contact with under normal conditions. I was beginning to make a good many friends whose conversation and outlook on life were interesting and new to me; I liked the scenery and the air, and — last not least — this place had become familiar to me and I distrusted change. I was prepared to pass quite a pleasant summer here, as far as a summer could be pleasant while the war went on.

Chapter IV
Some of the People

We were a motley crowd and there were some very surprising 'enemy aliens' amongst us; we were, in fact, quite cosmopolitan. One great friend of mine bore the name of Schulz — about as uncommon in Germany as that of Smith is in England. Schulz was very fond of me because I was about the only person he could talk to, for Schulz knew no language except Spanish. He was born in Mexico and looked a full-blooded Mexican Indio, but his name was Schulz, and so he had been arrested on board some ship and brought here. His mother, he told me, was Indian, he had never known his father, but his mother thought his name was Schulz and called her son after him. I am sure the good lady's memory must have been at fault. Schulz did not know his age, but he looked about twenty and had a very handsome, sullen sort of face and a feline body. He wore a khaki shirt and riding breeches which seemed an unusual outfit for a sailor, yet he was undoubtedly one for he exercised an art known to sailors only: all day long he sat on the ground and with a huge *navaja*[1] he carved minute full rigged ships which were miraculously introduced into bottles when finished. All other work he profoundly despised, nor did he attempt to sell his works of art; he had no needs of any sort. I tried to impress the fact on him that it would be extremely easy for him to be set free if he would take the trouble to explain his case and ask to be put in touch with his consulate, but he had no desire for freedom. Life could be far worse than this, he remarked, and that was undoubtedly true. He was a very wise child really, he had no needs, demanded nothing from life, did not bother about his fellow creatures or his surroundings. On the other hand he found great satisfaction in spitting frequently and adroitly: that was his way of expressing his opinion on the universe and on mankind.

Then there was an extremely black negro whose presence remained a mystery until Charlie managed to solve it. He discovered that the man knew Arabic, and got him to explain. He had been arrested on board a ship, and when asked his nationality had replied that he was a faithful son of the Caliph. That was all he knew, for the notion of nationality was unknown to uneducated Mahometans. The Caliph was, of course, the Sultan of Turkey, so he was imprisoned as a Turkish enemy alien. As a matter of fact he was an Egyptian and therefore (at that time) a British subject. Charlie explained this to him and got very excited about his case, but not so the negro! He only shook his head and said he knew what he had got but not what he might get, and Allah had ordained things for the best. White men, as is well known, are free from such fatalistic superstition, that is why 'Yankee' behaved very differently from these exotics. Yankee belonged to the rich, according to him to the fabulously wealthy. I don't know how he came to be there, I believe he had no papers or insufficient ones. He was

---

[1] A traditional Spanish folding-blade fighting and utility knife.

such a very typical son of the U.S.A. that the mistake seemed ludicrous. He did not know a word of German, had never been near that country, and had no sympathy with it whatsoever. In fact he loathed it now that the sinking of the *Lusitania* had landed him in this predicament. Nor was his opinion of the British very high just then. Yankee had a little of the Indian in his face and make, he was about twenty-five or so, tall, with lanky black hair, and disguised as a sort of cowboy, probably in order to demonstrate his Americanism. He wore silk shirts though. Mostly he was in a hell of a temper and extremely blasphemous — which was after all comprehensible — but he had a sense of humour all the same and told endless American jokes most of which were utterly silly. He lay all day full length in the sun and tried to sleep; then someone would tickle him and he would swear gorgeously. He got his release after a month and people were sorry to lose him. He had become quite popular.

The pride of our heart, however, remained with us: Billie. Billie was twenty-two, but looked eighteen and the most typical English boy one could find anywhere. Which is exactly what he was. He was just a jolly English schoolboy with an irresistible smile who quite saw the fun of the situation. He could not speak a word of any language but English, and as to Germany he hardly knew it existed. He had never seen a German before he came to Knockaloe, but he made friends with everyone and was adored by most, certainly by all the 90 percent who — as everywhere throughout the war — were bad 'haters.' Billie's parents had emigrated to Australia when he was quite a little boy, and they had died out there. He had studied architecture and was passing his summer holiday in Europe. When war broke out he was in Belgium and came to England at once — without a passport, for before the war hardly anyone ever troubled to take out a passport, and even less to take one with him when travelling. Billie landed in Southampton and thought some of the buildings of that port quite interesting. So he started sketching them, and was promptly arrested, for the interesting buildings happened to be part of the fortifications. He had no papers, so the authorities decided he could only be a German. I imagine that even they must have thought him and his sketching too naïve for a spy, but a German he would remain until he could prove another nationality, and so there he was amongst his 'compatriots.' He hoped to get his papers from Australia very soon, he told me, he had already waited ten months for them, meanwhile he intended to remain cheerful and did not despair of organizing football in the camp. Billie was not only popular on account of his charming smile, but also as a living proof of the utter lack of sense of the British authorities — which everyone felt they had shown in his own case as well — and because his presence consoled people in a way, for what could you expect if even Billie had been locked up! — I have often wondered if his papers ever arrived or what became of him.

One did not, however, have to turn to our 'exotics' to discover curious samples of humanity, plenty were to be found amongst those of undisputedly German nationality. The most striking figure of our crowd was a man who called himself Dr. A and was born in Berlin. He was an absolutely perfect example of the Bolshevik of popular imagery, a Bolshevik *avant la lettre*,[2] for in 1915 their existence was unknown to the world or, at any rate, the term meant nothing. It meant a good deal to this man, however, for he knew them all and corresponded with them, I believe. Before being interned he had, or said he had, lived in a sort of communist settlement in England. He was tall and very thin, he stooped and he had masses of untidy black hair covering his head and face. He looked like an unkempt and a little starved Assyrian king. His clothes, however, were not royal, for he invariably wore a pair of

---

[2] French: Before the letter, or rather, before the term Bolshevik came into common use.

old trousers over a bathing suit, and sandals. He would, in fact, have looked smartly dressed at Juan les Pins in the summer season of 1930, but in 1915 and in Knockaloe his was considered a scandalous get-up by nearly all his fellow prisoners. The doctor was an ardent revolutionary and he began his incendiary propaganda the very first day, which soon made him the best hated man there. The capitalist class was as furious with him, as might have been expected, but the majority did not take kindly either to his sharp tongue, his hissing and cutting voice, and his excessively Jewish appearance. As a convinced pacifist he condemned war and all the belligerents, no matter on which side they fought. He refused to make concessions to sentiment or patriotism; he was much too uncompromising and severe to gain popular applause. Strange to say, his only admirers were some very fair, very Teutonic sailors — at least it seemed very strange to me at the time, but when the revolution in Germany started by a sailors' revolt I began to see the connection between the two types, which in spite of all differences have one fundamental thing in common: love of independence. One very young, flaxen-haired sailor boy never left the doctor's side, and listened mute and adoring to all he said; I called him the John of this strange Christ who was perhaps more of a St. Paul. One could not help admiring his logic and his courage. He preached revolution by violence in all countries and was firmly convinced of the victory of communism, all of which seemed fantastic nonsense in 1915. Nor was the world he prophesied the one his hearers wished to look forward to. After victory and peace everyone was going to be happy and prosperous — that is what they hoped for (in common with the vast majority of people in all countries) and that is what they wished to hear. Some men — one never knew who they were — complained to the Commandant about the doctor's political speeches and meetings which, they said, created unrest in the camp. The Commandant sent for him and this is how the revolutionary described the interview: 'He looked at me, my beard, my naked shoulders, etc., with great disgust and said: "Do you consider this the proper costume to appear in here?" I said: "Certainly, why not?" He got furious and shouted: "You look like a wild beast," and I said, "You have put me in a cage like a wild beast, haven't you?" After that he laughed and said, "Well, there is something in that.'" He was transferred to another compound and so I lost sight of him, but I came across him again in 1918.

Another man I had noticed from the very beginning was one of the great number of Russo-Polish Jews from the East End, who were either born in the Polish provinces then forming part of Austria or Germany, or else were considered German on account of their names. In many cases they themselves were none too sure about their origin. This was a very small old man who looked more worn and weather-beaten than anything animate or inanimate I have ever seen. He was short, crooked and hunchbacked, wore a discoloured-looking red beard, and his skin looked like wrinkled parchment. His head leant against his right shoulder which made him look like a pensive crow. He wore a cutaway coat green with age and the remnants of a huge bowler hat, the crowning glory of which had almost departed. He was a passionate card-gambler like all his lot, and they spent their days quarrelling vociferously over very greasy cards, but he was also a very pious and strictly orthodox Jew as they all were. In fact, he was a hero, for for weeks on end he would only touch bread and water, and nearly starved. He and his friends were then transferred to a Kosher camp and the 'East End' disappeared from our community, which thereby lost much of its picturesqueness. But I had made his acquaintance long before that time. One could always find him at the pump before and after his 'meals,' muttering to himself incessantly while he performed the ablutions prescribed by the Law of Moses. Its followers must cleanse themselves before eating and after, and nothing would have made him shirk this obligation, so he held out a few fingers of first one hand and then the other, and sprinkled a few drops of water on them. To this cleansing rite he almost ran, all other cleansing he dispensed with and despised. Having exchanged a few remarks with him I asked him the usual question: 'What was your profession before you were interned?', for on that subject they all liked to discourse at length. His answer was: 'I watch corpses.' According to orthodox Jewish rite a corpse is honoured by watchers surrounding it until the time of the funeral, a pious duty performed by the nearest relatives. I did not know that professional watchers of that sort existed, but they do amongst the orthodox poor, for there may be no relatives or they may not have time to honour the dead for days. A very terrible profession it seemed to me, and one which no doubt only the poorest of the poor adopted. So I said with what I thought was tactful sympathy: 'That is not a very cheerful life for you, I am afraid.' His head quite touched his shoulder as he looked up at me angrily. 'Not cheerful, what do you mean by not cheerful? — I like it!' He turned to go, but thought better of it; he came quite near to me and said almost triumphantly as it were: 'I like to do the talking. They don't talk back.' After which this most Shakespearean character I have come across in my life left me and restarted his endless muttered monologue.

In those early days of imprisonment there was far more mutual tolerance than in later times when people's nerves were edged and frayed. Later it would have been impossible for men of such different classes and customs, for such contradictory types to live together almost peaceably, but in 1915 there was as yet no sense of duration, internment was looked on as an abnormal episode, not as a mode of existence of possibly endless length. In 1915 people were still full of hope and convinced that the war was approaching its end. If they did not really believe — as some of them professed to — that a huge fleet of Zeppelins was coming to liberate all the prisoners, they were sure that the fall of Warsaw which had just taken place was the beginning of the end. And anyone who would not share that conviction was looked on with great disfavour, if not suspicion.

Chapter V
Huts, Hill and Hospital

After about a fortnight I began to feel restless. I had got to know all the people who seemed worthwhile, I was getting tired of lying in the sun all day, I wanted to work. I had, in the last few years before the war, evolved a peculiar kind of miniature painting and lost interest in all realistically representative work. These paintings were done on parchment, a Chinese ink line drawing serving as a basis for glowing colour-schemes of pure purples, blues, reds, etc., with a good deal of silver and gold. They were Oriental in inspiration and the technique influenced by Persian miniature painting, but what they represented was purely my own, a mass of fantasies often unintelligible even to myself. I had always surrounded this work with quite a ritual: I had to feel in the proper mood for it (which generally meant the early morning hours), all had to be quiet around me; I used a certain table, certain pens or brushes only, and I preferred a certain room to work in. How could I take up my work here! But I felt I must try, for I could not bear empty idleness any longer, it would drive me insane. So, rather desperately, I made my first attempt. The hut had but one table and its inmates sat round it every evening, all day in wet weather (we were getting some rainy days then) and half the day in fine weather. They talked, they read, they quarrelled, they played cards. That was the worst, for they heartily banged their cards on the table, and the table shook. If I was just doing a stroke with my pen or putting on a spot of colour with my brush they would go astray if the table shook, and if a single one went astray the picture was done for, for nothing can be erased or altered on parchment. But I managed, for I felt I had to manage because it meant such a lot to me; it meant that I could continue my inner life in spite of all outer circumstances, it meant defying the world to do its worst — and God knows what failure would have meant to me. So I managed to work, some days at least. I sat there waiting till the table was stable again after a shock and — what was more trying — stopping work when a shock was to be foreseen. Some men were interested in what I was doing, some even refrained voluntarily from banging the table, but such proofs of goodwill were rare. The atmosphere of Knockaloe was changing rapidly, relations had already begun to get strained. The moneyless distrusted all the moneyed and suspected them of working their own ends by bribery and corruption, but they were by no means united amongst themselves. The sailors loathed the waiters and barbers: 'You're a lot of pimps,' one red-haired sailor assured them every evening, and enlarged at length on the subject. But to the waiters, etc., the sailors were uneducated brutes. Nor was the more opulent minority united any longer, they had first split on the question of the 'anarchist orator,' their politics divided them, the warlike fire-eaters hated the more level-headed or pacifist who in their turn despised them. The camp was breaking up into hostile factions. As soon as it rained the clay soil became impassable, everyone sheltered inside the hut and there was quarrelling going on between some people or other nearly all the time. They had nothing else to do, poor things, but grumble or quarrel! They hated the camp by now, they knew that release was out of the question, but the advantages of other camps assumed ever greater proportions in their imaginations. Wakefield in particular became a name to conjure with, and life there a prolonged weekend party at some great country mansion. But of course, one would never get there, and I gave it little thought, though I had put my name on the list of those who desired to go there on that first day in Knockaloe which already seemed infinitely removed. I still thought Knockaloe quite pleasant when the sun shone; we were now marched twice a week to a hill close by which had been surrounded by wire and was to serve as a playground. There was real grass there, a wide view, splendid air. All sorts of games were played; football of sorts, I remember, amongst others, and that hill is the birthplace of German boxing. Boxing was unknown in Germany before the war, the first boxing lessons to some of the future professionals were given there by men who had learnt it in England. Yes, in fine weather it was not a bad place, but it rained very frequently now, it poured outside, it was damp inside the lightly built huts; the moisture came up through the badly joined boards of the floor. I caught a bad cold.

One morning I awoke with what must have been very high fever. I was too dazed to realize what was happening as I was carried out of the hut on a stretcher, but when I did realize my surroundings I discovered myself in the Camp Hospital, of which I had heard awful tales. I suppose I had *grippe* though that name, which covers so many diseases and symptoms the doctors do not understand and cannot cure, did not come into use until the epidemic of 1918, which killed more people than the war had done. I was given aspirin, and on the second day I felt fully conscious again and well enough to get interested in my new surroundings. Being in hospital was truly much worse than being in one's accustomed hut. It was a hut like all the others, only it had a WC at one end. It contained two parallel rows of beds and nothing else. It lay on a road outside the compound though inside the camp, and its inmates were allowed no intercourse with anyone outside the hospital. There was at that time (things may have changed later) one solitary doctor or medical officer to look after the health of all the thousands of prisoners. Needless to say, he was terribly overworked and had no time to attend to individual cases that were not extremely urgent. The nursing of the patients and the care of the ward were left to a number of men chosen from such prisoners as had been *Heilgehiljen*, that is to say, barber-surgeons, or who pretended to some experience of nursing. Their control and power over the sick was as good as unlimited, for when the doctor paid one of his rapid visits one of these men would accompany him on his round, serve as an interpreter and prevent direct communication. That, at least, was what the sick man in the bed next to mine told me when the 'nurse' had left the room. The poor fellow, a sailor, was terribly ill with some disease of the bones which necessitated operations impossible to perform there. He had lain there for weeks waiting to be moved to an operating hospital and he had lost all hope. Maybe that his was really a hopeless case and that there would have been no object in moving him and operating on him, but that was what he had been told and what he believed, and so he lay there cursing all: the people who had made the war, the English who were letting him rot and die; but worst of all he hated the nurses. 'What is the matter with you?' he asked me. 'Nothing much,' I said, 'I shall go back to the camp in a day or two.' He stared at me and started a loud and prolonged laugh. 'You go back tomorrow!' he cried, 'you will be here a good long time, believe me.' 'But why?' I asked in surprise. 'Because you have money,' he explained as if he were talking to a child. One's life there, he said, was unbearable if one had no money, they just took no notice of you at all. Every little service had to be paid for. But the moneyed were few, therefore they were very precious to the nurses, and their one idea was to keep them there as long as ever possible. As to the doctor, it was no use counting on him, even if one could talk to him (many of them knew no English) there was no chance of doing so; he just heard the report of the nurse, told him what to do and went on. 'You can believe me,' he said, 'you will live here while the war lasts and I shall die here long before it is over.' Imaginings of a diseased brain? Possibly. I tried the nurse in the evening. 'I am quite well enough to go back to my compound again,' I said, 'I would like to go tomorrow.' 'That is quite out of the question, you are much too ill,' he said curtly and went away. I thought the matter over during a restless night, and the next morning I got up and dressed — which did not worry the nurse at all. Then I went and stood outside the hospital — which one was allowed to do to get fresh air, and leant against the wall. I had decided to wait for the doctor, and after I had waited five hours or more I saw him approaching and walked up to him. 'I am quite well, again,' I said, 'and would like to return to my compound. I have had a little fever, but it has quite gone now.' 'In that case you may go back,' he said indifferently. 'Would you be kind enough to give me a written order,' I asked, 'it is apparently not easy to leave this place without one.' He gave me a quick look, but he asked no questions — poor fellow, he had enough to worry him, no doubt, without going out of his way for more trouble. He scribbled something on a piece of paper and gave it me. I thanked him and went back to lie on my bed. When the nurse came round in the afternoon I casually remarked 'I am going back to my camp tonight.' He grinned sarcastically: 'You don't say so! Quite a mistake, I think.' 'Hardly,' I replied, showing him the precious scrap of paper. He was furious but impotent: 'Well,' he said gruffly, 'what are you waiting for?' 'Only for the pleasure of your company, because you have to accompany me to the gate, you know.' I said farewell to the poor sailor and promised to do my best for him. I don't know whether it was due to my agitation, but apparently he was sent off to be operated on a few days later — though I never heard what the result had been. I left my most unwilling companion at the gates of my compound. I felt — absurdly — that I was once more free and I prayed but for one thing: never to be ill again in camp! I met all my camp acquaintances as if they were most intimate friends from whom I had been separated for years; I was overjoyed to be back amongst them; I was grateful for what seemed freedom, security, and human fellowship by comparison.

After that interlude I should probably have been quite happy at Knockaloe for a good long time, but fate had decided otherwise. I had only been back a few days when a list was published giving the names of the prisoners whose desire to go to Wakefield had been granted, and my name was on that list. There were sixty in all, and fifty-nine of them were overjoyed at their good luck. But I felt curiously depressed. We instantly became objects of envy and hatred to all others, and I was almost inclined to share their point of view. I felt I was leaving them in the lurch, that there should not have been 'gentlemen's camps.' I felt great regret at tearing myself away from Knockaloe. All of which was no doubt illogical and sentimental, but the fact remains all the same. At Wakefield the men who had come with me from Knockaloe were furious with me for speaking almost tenderly of that place, for it is part of the psychology of internment camps to consider anyone a 'traitor' who finds anything but martyrdom in any of its aspects.

Much envied, greeted by few, sullenly ignored by most the sixty passed out the gates of Knockaloe Camp the following morning, and the second journey into the unknown began.

Chapter VI
The Journey to Wakefield, and a Surprise

It was a fine day and we marched for miles. It seemed very strange to see fields, houses, animals, even normal and quite uninterned and unmilitary human beings in the distance. One had almost forgotten the existence of such everyday life and conditions. The scenery was charming — I was sorry to have to get into a train for Douglas at some wayside station. Douglas again looked pleasant enough in the sunshine, but one was rushed to the steamer bound for Liverpool. We had a calm, uneventful crossing; we were allowed on deck this time. Everyone was in high spirits, this was indeed wonderful. But evidently strong contrasts were considered good for us. In going out to the Isle the journey had begun well and ended badly, and now again we were in for an abrupt change. From the steamer we were bundled into police vans, known to the populace as 'Black Marias' and used for the transport of criminals. One tried to joke about it, but one did not really feel much like joking, for quite apart from the discomfort — those horrible hard benches and want of ventilation — it seemed a gratuitous insult. Next to me sat a black-bearded man whom I had never seen before and he began a conversation by saying, 'How very different these vans are from the type used in London, are they not?' I did not encourage further conversation. There was a hostile crowd at the station gates, it seemed like Stratford all over again; at last we were seated in the train, but there was not much cheeriness left by this time, all were mute and depressed. Evening was coming, the train steamed slowly through a black factory district. Houses, chimneys, blast furnaces, clouds and gloom, and I thought longingly of the pure sky left behind. What would this new place be like? Discussions had begun again, some of the men knew all about it. It would be a marvellous place. Lofthouse Park was its name, not Wakefield, that was only the nearest city, but Lofthouse Park was a large estate with a mansion on it. Would we live in real rooms? Not only that, but everyone had a room to himself, there were gardens and a park, there was — one had read in the papers — a golf course. A gentlemen's camp, you understand, they said. It was strange to reflect that a few months ago one could have taken treatment as a gentleman for granted — was there any other possibility? Well, there had been crowds, hospitals, Black Marias since then. Perhaps all that was over now and one would be allowed to live more or less like one had been used to, though with restrictions of liberty of movement. Why shouldn't it be true, after all? Why should one be punished, what wrong had one done, was it not enough to restrict one's movements to a country estate if one's mixing with Englishmen was considered undesirable and dangerous? It seemed plausible enough.

We got out of the train, walked through steep streets. There was a large church — I thought of the *Vicar of Wakefield*. More steep streets, workmen's cottages in serried rows, a smoky sky, a stiff climb, and then — barbed wire once more. Another gate, another camp. Smaller than Knockaloe, red corrugated iron huts instead of wooden huts, sand instead of clay. No hills, no sea. A dirty, empty hut. Night. The most hopeless night since that first night at Stratford, which seemed so infinitely far removed already.

I did not see the camp until the following morning, but its discovery was not a pleasant surprise as had been that of Knockaloe. The disappointment had been too great.

At one time Lofthouse Park had been — as it survived in the legends I had heard — a country house surrounded by fine grounds. The house could still be seen, a simple Georgian mansion surrounded by fine old trees, and it was now the abode of the Commandant — unfortunately however, house and lawns were separated from the camp by barbed wire. The grounds had, I suppose, been sold a number of years ago and a sort of amusement park had sprung up there. A large wooden building, built for a concert hall or theatre, had formed its centre and that had been used to house prisoners and become the nucleus of the camp. There were now three camps, each containing about five hundred men and — heaven knows why — separated from each other by barbed wire. The first camp was that which had arisen round the concert hall, the South Camp. The hall, which contained a stage and an auditorium, had become a rabbit warren full of beds, chairs, clothes, and men. Some wooden huts had been added when it overflowed, hospital barracks had followed, a few trees remained. The South Camp was pleasantly irregular and untidy; it could, by a stretch of imagination, pass for picturesque. After the South Camp the North Camp had been built, and it was as correctly planned and hopeless as regulations prescribed. Long, low, wooden huts stood in serried rows and there was a corrugated iron hall presented by an Anglo-German donor. The ground was flat and there was a fairly large free space for games and exercise. The West Camp, built on sloping ground, was the latest and smallest. It had corrugated iron huts, and was a treeless, grassless, sandy waste. It was this we had exchanged for Knockaloe, and it looked the most hopeless, ugliest and gloomiest place to me on my first morning there. Only remnants of what had been an avenue of fine chestnut trees, outside the wire, of course, were pleasant to look at. The camp was not only hideous but also much smaller than the 'compound' at Knockaloe had been, as it was intended for only half the number of prisoners. All it was, was an uglier and smaller cage of exactly the same description!

But the fact that it was to be a more comfortable cage became apparent almost at once. At that time, in 1915, prisoners were allowed to buy most things they could pay for, and the tradesmen of the neighbouring town of Leeds did not scruple to take advantage of that fact. When a new batch of prisoners arrived, a Leeds firm sent up a cart full of the furnishings that might be required, and thus I became possessed of a camp bed, stuff for curtains, and even a tin jug and basin. Boards and other necessities entered the camp in some mysterious manner; there were carpenters amongst the prisoners, and there was a certain measure of freedom in the arrangement of your surroundings. The canteen seemed a sort of Selfridge's after that at Knockaloe, so large was the variety of its goods, and there even existed a kind of snack counter with all sorts of German *Delikatessen* and glasses of sherry or beer. That seemed extremely luxurious, worthy of a 'gentlemen's camp.'

Wakefield provided me with the only simple and straightforward definition of that mysterious creature, the gentleman. To the authorities responsible for its creation a gentleman was a man prepared to pay ten shillings a week to them for the privilege of being there. He was allowed to draw £3 per week from his deposit (if any) at the Camp Bank, and to spend them inside the camp or on things ordered from the outer world (all this was to change later). He could have books or anything else, except foodstuffs or objects considered dangerous, sent from the outside world, and his friends in England — if he had any — could send him what they liked. Once a week a firm of Leeds hosiers displayed their goods in the camp and they must have made a lot of money, for here in Wakefield everyone was decently and conventionally clad, as gentlemen should be. There was a P.O., there was a barber's shop, there was presently a hut given by the Y.M.C.A. (for that association and the Quakers were the only ones to stick to their notions of Christian conduct even in wartime). Wakefield was, in fact, an extremely civilized and comfortable place when compared to Knockaloe. All the newcomers were already delighted with the change and congratulating each other on their lucky escape. My three taxi friends, for instance, seemed quite happy. We had already begun the construction of our 'home.' It was divided off from the rest of the hut by curtains of blue casement cloth, held the beds, and soon some sort of cupboard and a table, to which I added a small bookshelf. I was very pleased with so much comfort and beauty, but I did not feel happy — a fact I took good care to keep to myself. Knockaloe had been a Wild West place, rough, barbaric, but, to me at least, exhilarating. I had always known that its interest lay in the presence of what I have called the 90 percent, yet I had never reflected on what a camp might be without their presence. What would life in this new place be like where all were gentlemen, with the exception of a very limited number of stewards, etc. It seemed to me a very colourless, very drab and monotonous place. I might be wrong, of course — all the others liked it. It might be that the change of air affected me, it seemed so heavy and listless here. But one would get used to the climate, that was nothing. It was not the physical atmosphere that mattered, but the mental atmosphere — what would that gentlemanly atmosphere turn out to be like?

Chapter VII
Barbed Wire Air

The process of adaptation to new and difficult surroundings had taken up the first weeks in Knockaloe, the repetition of that process in Wakefield took me many months. Possibly one had already lost some of one's elasticity, but in my case this new adaptation was in itself more difficult because I was entirely out of sympathy with my new surroundings. Knockaloe in its early days, which were the days I knew there, was restless, seething, and anarchical; it was very rough but it was also very alive and stimulating; it was dynamic. Wakefield had settled into a routine long before I knew it and that routine continued in endless monotony for ever after; it was static. Wakefield in fact was dead. Dostoevsky in his marvellous memories of his life as a prisoner in Siberia calls the prison 'a house of the dead,' and no better term could be found for Wakefield. That book describes its atmosphere most admirably, and even most of the characters depicted are images of Wakefield prisoners; like causes led to like results.

Wakefield was an extremely orderly place, as orderly, monotonous and drab as a lower middle-class suburb, but it was a suburb without a city, and its inhabitants suburbanites out of work. Everything was organized, everything ordered. The huts had captains, the captains a chief-captain, and he an adjutant with so little sense of humour that he actually signed himself Adjutant L. and wished to be addressed by his ridiculous title. There were committees for everything, and nearly everyone was a member of one or the other or had some sort of post in the P.O. or the kitchen department or God knows what, and they all took themselves and their activities most seriously. Nearly all took part or desired to take part in the government and administration of this place where there was nothing to govern, as the real governing powers were outside the camp, and there was little enough to administer. It was and became ever more an administration which served no purpose except that of giving its participants a feeling of their own importance, it was full of corruption and protectionism. If anyone benefited by it, it was the real administration of the camp, the British military in command. Whenever in later life people asked one what that existence had been like their first question was invariably: 'Were you treated well?' It would have been difficult to make them understand that the treatment by the military authorities (which their question referred to) was really a very minor matter once the fact of imprisonment had been accepted. There was so very little of it. Soldiers kept guard to prevent prisoners escaping, officers counted their heads twice daily, anonymous authorities issued orders which were mostly restrictive and irritating, and that was all. During my stay in Wakefield there were three or four different commandants, but I cannot say that I noticed any difference whatsoever in the treatment of the prisoners. Very likely things were different in other camps or in other countries; I don't wish to make any general statement, and I believe that all general statements about no matter what aspect of the war are nonsensical. I am not prepared to say what British treatment of prisoners of war or of interned civilians was — fair, correct, brutal, inhuman, indifferent — I can only speak of my own experience and that was that the treatment of prisoners was standardized and carried out according to War or Home Office rules and regulations. Either these left no room for personal initiative or else no advantage was taken of existing possibilities, but certainly there was no personal contact between prisoners and gaolers and therefore no like or dislike. The prisoners, of course, professed hatred of their oppressors, but it was really half-hearted and none too sincere, just part of that prescribed hatred of the enemy which had become universal. A prisoners' camp is in many ways similar to a school, and schoolboys do not hate the legislators of compulsory education, but their masters or fellows, and what they suffer most from are not the restrictions of their state but the treatment meted out to them by the other boys. When I look back on the years spent in camp, from 1915 to 1918, I cannot recall a single instance of cruelty or of kindness to me from officers or soldiers. Many of the orders enforced were, I consider, cruel, and many more were quite absurd, but that was the fault of the system, not of the men who might as well have been machines set going. The system was cruel as must be all systems which do not aim at justice; it did not treat or profess to treat people according to their deserts, it was guided by entirely different considerations. The Germans in England, the foreigners of enemy nations in all countries, must not be allowed to join the belligerent forces of their countries of origin and they must not be allowed to endanger the safety of the countries they happened to have been in when war broke out. They were therefore rounded up and locked away in camps because that was the easiest way of dealing with the problem. As a sop to certain qualms of conscience (for thousands of these prisoners had friends who knew them as harmless or likable people) each government gave out that they were only following the enemies' example. That sufficed as an explanation of anything during the war, and that fact I consider the worst aspect of war mentality. That two wrongs *do* make a right became the accepted moral teaching of all nations, and reprisals a term which excused any crime. And if it happened that one party had no knowledge of what the other really had done, it acted on rumours. In no previous European war had enemy civilians been interned; in 1914 every country interned them and every country gave out that the measure adopted was one of reprisal for similar treatment of their own subjects. The way prisoners were treated varied on that same principle of reprisals. When prisoners at Wakefield complained to the neutral representative who sometimes visited the camp of insufficient nourishment they were told that the 'number of calories' had been reduced to correspond to that given to British prisoners in Germany, and the British there were no doubt told the same tale. If a French city was bombarded by German aeroplanes and women and children killed, then the French bombarded a German city (or more if possible), killing German women and children, and everyone (not quite everyone, to be just) applauded them. No considerations of humanity need deter the governments or fighting forces of the nations from any measure whatsoever, and they did not; but it was always better to convince one's own people that the enemies had been the first to employ any particularly nauseous weapon and that your side was merely taking reprisals. During the war no one could ascertain the truth of such a statement and after the war no one would care.

That, in short, was the origin and the reason of the cruelty of the system of treatment; its absurdity was due to the red tape and utter lack of comprehension inherent in all administrative measures and intensified by the war spirit prevalent. In this, however, the system of treatment of prisoners did not vary in principle from the system of treatment of the nation's own subjects. The first were bundled into camps, the latter into the armies; both to be ruled by systems and regulations, both to be treated as numbers, both to suffer from reprisals for deeds and actions on which they had not been consulted. And as the war progressed, restrictions and coercion gradually enslaved all the civilian population as well, until all the world seemed to lie under the shadow of the words *Es ist verboten*, once supposed to be the true and exclusive expression of Prussianism.

That, then, was the law under which one lived, unchangeable for the time being as a law of nature, and therefore accepted after a short resistance as something inevitable. That law had its executants, and they again were accepted as inevitable. I maintain that after a time they ceased to trouble the prisoners (until some new change for the worse occurred) and that they really gave very little thought to them. Unconsciously they classed them with other necessary evils: cold, disease, death, bereavement, which one deplores but takes for granted. They represented the peculiar form in which war affected prisoners, and war itself was a fact, a sort of unending earthquake from which there was no escape.

This long digression is intended to clear up a misconception of the essential character of life in internment camps shared by everyone I have ever met who had had no personal experience of it. They believe that the interned had 'a good time' (comparatively) when they were 'treated well' and 'a bad time' when they were 'treated badly.' But if bad treatment might have aggravated and good treatment eased the prisoner's lot, neither one nor the other could change its essentials or even modify them to any considerable extent. The evil was inherent in the system and in the way that system affected and changed the prisoners. When people asked me whether I had been badly treated I truthfully said 'No,' but when they continued and said: 'Then you didn't have too bad a time' — which seemed the only logical conclusion — the answer should have been 'I had an awful time,' or perhaps, in my own case, 'I had what you would consider an awful time.'

But that would have led to lengthy explanations and one was as disinclined to talk much of one's experiences as were the soldiers back from the front. Things are different now, twelve years have passed, and one has gained sufficient distance for dispassionate judgment. That, I think, explains the great number of war books written lately and the great success of many of them: the writers feel that they can now write the truth (as it appears to them, for there is no absolute truth and no general truth in such matters) and the public is eager to learn the truth, having realized that what they were told about the war while it was in progress or shortly after it was over bore but a faint resemblance to any sort of truth.

The whole problem of prisoners of war and their treatment was a secondary consideration in all countries while all energies were directed towards winning the war, and the fate and treatment of interned civilians again was but a small and none too important part of that problem, yet a good deal of space was given to it in the papers and in parliamentary discussions. There were two main sides to it; the British public wished to know how their men were being treated in enemy countries, to be reassured about their fate, and to urge the Government to do all in its power to improve their lot. That was the one side; the other was the question of how enemy prisoners were being treated in Britain, and that could not be separated from the first. I do not know how near the truth were the statements about conditions and treatment of British prisoners abroad, but I do know that the picture of conditions and treatment of prisoners in British internment camps given to the public was extremely fanciful. That whole question had become part of the vast system of propaganda attributed, rightly or wrongly, to Lord Northcliffe.[1] The main idea never varied: British prisoners abroad

---

1 Alfred Charles William Harmsworth, 1st Viscount Northcliffe, owner of the *Daily Mail* and many of the most widely-read newspapers in Great Britain during the First World War.

were being treated abominably, German prisoners in England were being treated with foolish generosity. The latter was, to be just, frequently denied in parliament by members of the Government, but this made no difference whatsoever to the continuation of the press campaign against that supposed scandal. There were very few days when the more sensational papers (we got all the English papers, but no foreign ones) did not contain a paragraph under the (invariable) heading: 'Our pampered Huns' and the statements they contained were not mere travesties of truth but simply fantasies. I have read descriptions of dinners (including full menu) which never took place, of prisoners disporting themselves on a golf course which never existed, of strange happenings between prisoners and women friends who visited them, when in reality officers and soldiers on guard were present on all such occasions, and there were countless other inventions which I have forgotten. Wakefield was their favourite aim of attack, being a 'privileged' camp, together with Donnington Hall which was an officers' camp. There is no need to speak of the impression these accounts made on the minds of the prisoners, but the impression produced on the British public was, of course, such as was desired: they were perhaps mildly angry with the Government, but at the same time not displeased with such a show of characteristically British magnanimity, and any possible sympathy they might have felt with the prisoners was killed outright. How far that propaganda impressed the neutrals, which was always one of its main aims, I do not know, but my own opinion is that at least the European neutral powers ceased to be impressed by any propaganda of either side after a very few months and got bored with the absolutely contradictory statements screamed at them day after day. But as far as the British public went that question was settled. One must remember what a small minority reads the better-class papers which did not join in that particular chorus and how vast a majority the others. The millions knew the truth as they thought: German prisoners in England, interned civilians in particular, were not only treated well, but with quixotic generosity, whereas the treatment of British prisoners in Germany was cruel and barbarous. And all the time the real truth which was never told them was that the treatment in both countries was as nearly identical as circumstances allowed, that both sides were continually receiving reports about the camps from neutral observers and hastened to adjust the conditions they controlled to those reported from the other side. Exceptions to this rule there may have been, there were probably remote camps seldom or possibly never visited by neutrals, and — as we had cause to know — these neutral inspections remained very much on the surface, but such details cannot change the dominating facts. What happened to the prisoners on one side happened to those on the other, and their lot was subject to a system of mutual reprisals from which the authorities dreamt as little of abstaining as — to choose a well-known example — the flying forces refrained from 'punitive expeditions.' But the British public read with horror and loathing that 'the Germans have bombarded the unfortified town of ——' and later with satisfaction 'we have bombarded places of strategical importance behind the enemies lines'; while the German public was given the same news in the inversed terms. Thus, as Georg Brandes had foreseen from the very beginning, Truth was murdered by War and thus every day that hatred was fanned anew without which the war could not have continued.

Chapter VIII
Barbed Wire Sickness

I had been interned in June, but it was only two months later, at Wakefield, that I realized what had happened. Proust in *A la Recherche du temps perdu* gives a very lucid explanation of the difference between knowing a fact and realizing it; the intellect knows that some event has happened, but it may be very long after that that event is emotionally apprehended, realized. For a long time I had simply considered I was living under abnormal circumstances, was passing through an interruption of my normal existence which I would soon take up again, but now it dawned on me that the abnormal had become the permanent, the normal. One must remember that there was absolutely no limit to be foreseen to the duration of the war and of my imprisonment, nor could one know to what one would then return, if one lived to return to anything. It was gradually becoming clear that the old order of things had passed away, and that what had been, what one had left, would never be found again. The past was dead, the future, if there should be a future, was a blank, there was nothing left but the present, and my present was the life of a prisoner. I realized my situation and I realized as if it had been quite new to me that it was horrible and that I detested it. But it is very difficult to explain why it was horrible, if it is comparatively easy to explain — as I have already begun to do in the preceding chapter — where its horror did not lie. It did not lie in the fact of being caged behind barbed wire. Speaking for myself, I find that one got used to that fact pretty soon and that it ceased to worry one. It became a matter of habit, one took it for granted. The world ceased at the barbed wire, and what lay outside it might as well have belonged to a different planet. A monk gets used to limiting his world to the precincts of his monastery, an invalid to those of his sickroom, a prisoner to those of his prison. It is not an easy resignation, but it does not present an insurmountable difficulty. Nor was the horror due to the treatment of the prisoners by their warders. Naturally this was what the prisoners' thoughts dwelt on most, or at least what they complained about most bitterly and most frequently, just as schoolboys will attribute all their ills to the masters. And these men of mature age were indeed being treated, restricted, and punished for offences like schoolboys. There were doubtless many quite unnecessary hardships, but there again — one got used to them. To me, at any rate, their absurdity was much more vivid than their cruelty. It was all so grotesque! You could not pass through the barbed wire from one camp to another without the accompaniment of bayonets — that portly suburban watchmaker had suddenly become so alarmingly dangerous that his every step had to be guarded by heavily armed soldiers day and night. The censorship was grotesque: the prisoners there had nothing of any interest to write to anybody, and what could it matter what anyone wrote to them, but one must not allude to the war nor criticize conditions in the camp. Anything except 'I hope this finds you as it leaves me' was fraught with danger, it appeared. The 'parades' were grotesque, at which twice daily the men were assembled before their huts to be counted. There was one quite amiable old captain who could never count right. He pointed his finger at each head in turn and hopefully announced a wrong number. The 'captain' corrected him most respectfully: 'Twenty-one, sir' (for heaven's sake don't forget the 'sir') and the poor man started again. First there had been too few, now there were too many, and in the end he accepted the proposed number and passed on to a similar performance at the next hut. There were fifteen such huts in our camp whose inmates had thus to be counted twice daily while the war lasted. It was grotesque to have to sit in the dark after 10 p.m.; it was altogether grotesque to treat grown-up men as children and civilians as captured soldiers. But all that was just part of a military system which was — as a rule — executed by its servants without particular malice and ill will. It was not any more amusing or less ridiculous for that man to have to count us than for us to be counted, for the guards to have to stand and to shout 'Number ten (or whatever it was) and all's well' every half hour during the night than for us to be woken by their hoarse and warlike cries. I think the censor must have thought his job pretty absurd, and I don't imagine that the man with the bayonet who prevented me from endangering the safety of the realm during my passage between barbed wires of different labels felt particularly heroic. I did not see that their lot was very much happier than ours and I could not bear them any grudge. The whole thing was an abomination, a neo-barbarism. Originally there had been some sense in it: the Government had interned those whom they knew to be, or believed to be, dangerous, and they had to be guarded. But later on, as a result of press campaigns, of nervousness, of some people's vindictiveness or else by way of reprisal (this excuse was, of course, adopted by both sides) they had laid their hands on many thousands whom they knew to be perfectly harmless people of a type which in all previous European wars had been left alone. 'To be interned or segregated for their own safety' they had declared. Then why not have sent them to some remote part of the country to live in? That was done in France where the treatment was much more varied: better in some cases, very much worse in others. Why separate them from their wives and children? Why, in short, deliver them to the military authorities and treat them as prisoners of war? There was no justification for all this, but there was a reason: it was much the simplest thing to do. There were so many more important matters to think about for government and governed; compulsory service had come, everyone had to put up with compulsion in some form or other, it was war. The civilian prisoners were an uncomfortable sideshow and, at a time when numbers were everything, not important enough to bother about. That is, I imagine, what the governments of all the various fatherlands really felt about the matter. What did twenty or thirty thousand men matter when one counted in millions! So one put them in barbed wire cages and forgot about them.

But it was a crime against twenty or thirty thousand human beings, a crime against human personality and that was what one felt. No one person in particular was responsible for it — who, indeed, was ever responsible for anything in the war if one went deep enough into the matter? Should one 'hate' the commandant who obeyed orders, or the War Office (that very ugly building) or that abstract, the British nation? Apparently some people could hate abstractions. 'The only good German is a dead German' was a phrase some papers repeated with gusto, but mine is not a generalizing mind. Many years later, Mr. Lloyd George (so strong on 'hanging the Kaiser' in 1918) remarked that in 1914 all the different countries and governments 'had slithered into war,' and in just the same way they had slithered into their internment policy as I very clearly realized from the very beginning. Thus it was not the fact of being imprisoned which was horrible, for as I have explained imprisonment *per se* is no more than restriction of movement and that one gets used to in time. What was horrible was that one had ceased to be an individual and had become a number. One ceased to be oneself, an individual free to act and responsible for his actions and for his actions alone. What I mean when I say, 'I suddenly realized what had happened,' is that I realized that I was no longer I, an entity, but a small particle of a whole, of an undesired community, called The Camp. Some man I do not even know by sight transgresses some regulation or other and the camp is punished for it, I am punished for it — for I am no longer I. He is found outside his hut after 10 p.m. without valid excuse and I am forbidden to write letters for a week or to receive parcels. I may be as perfect a sample of what the ideal interned civilian should be, but that won't help me at all, I am at the mercy of what any other of the fifteen hundred ex-individuals here may see fit to do or to omit, besides depending on ever possible freaks of temper of those in authority. That loss of personal responsibility is the first horrible feature of internment life and it is extremely demoralizing in the long run, for it kills one's sense of responsibility in the end. If I am responsible for everybody else's deeds, well then, everybody else is responsible for mine, and not I in particular; and what I do can be no more my fault than what anybody else does if I am equally punished for one or the other. I don't commit a crime: the camp does. All education from the tenderest age on tries to implant that sense of personal responsibility in the mind of human beings (even in that of dogs and cats), internment life undoes what education has built up in years of struggle, or rather in many centuries of effort.

It will be said that this is not peculiar to internment life and that it is one of the most striking and general effects of war. I am absolutely of that opinion, and it bears out what I said about the powers responsible for internment: the effect of war is to create an abnormal state in which no one can be honestly considered responsible for his actions. Is a private responsible — no, he obeys somebody's orders who obeys somebody else's orders until you come to a figurehead who does not know the orders given because they are details far beneath his personal consideration — and so no one is responsible, but anyone may be punished if things go wrong. No, this consequence of the war-spirit is not peculiar to internment camps, what is peculiar to them is, however, the fact that the prisoners there are incessantly and without a minute's respite in that position of helpless interdependency; there is no leave, there is no 'behind the line,' there is no dismissal. They share this particular horror of war in an aggravated form.

But there are plenty of other horrors peculiar to their state alone, just as there are plenty of others peculiar to those who suffered from the war in a different way from theirs. Most of the interned would, had they been free, have seen active service; through being interned they were spared all danger, all the terrors that fell to the lot of the soldiers. To my mind the lot of the soldier was infinitely the worse of the two, for I do not pretend to be a hero and I have a very deep-rooted prejudice against bloodshed, but many of my fellow prisoners thought differently. There were in all countries very many prisoners who tried to escape in order to fight, just as there certainly were many soldiers who preferred being taken prisoners. There is no sense in comparing the disadvantages of one state with those of the other, more particularly if you only know one of the two by personal experience, and my object is to speak only of those I have known, and which have, I think, remained unfamiliar to the general public.

Soldiers led a dangerous and terrible life, prisoners led a helpless and senseless one. Soldiers fought, they were active, they had an aim. They were protecting their country, they were trying to achieve an object, they felt (the great majority felt this, I think) that they were doing something indispensable and very praiseworthy, and all was done to strengthen that conviction in them. The interned civilians were doing nothing, were completely useless. They were quite passive, they suffered in their way, but their suffering was of no use to anybody, nor were they glorified for it. They were quite helpless and quite superfluous, their existence was utterly aimless, their lives perfectly futile. That sense of *complete futility* is the second great horror of internment life. One day these men had been torn from their homes, from their occupations and interests and put in a cage for no purpose but to wait months, a year, many years, till the end of their lives — who knew — until war should be over. There to do what they pleased, provided it was of no earthly use to anybody. The British, of course, could not allow anything that might help the Germans, the Germans interdicted all work of any kind as it might be helpful to the British. They were there with no object whatsoever in view, they just had to wait and wait and wait.

And, strange as it may appear, impossible as it appeared in the first few months, one gets used even to that. One gets used to it because time is a mirage. Time passes slowly when days are full of activities, that is to say after a few very varied days a long time seems to have passed. If you are travelling about, seeing many cities, sights, people, in a few weeks it will seem to you as if you had travelled for months; if, on the other hand, you spend the same number of days in great monotony, let us say lying on the sands and gazing at the sea, time will seem to have passed very quickly. And if you get the incredible sameness and monotony of a prisoner's life, what happens is not so much that time seems short (a day may seem endless) but that you lose all count, all sensation of time. *Time stands still*. Days, weeks, months, years, all these artificial divisions follow each other in endless monotony, time has ceased to have any signification; where there is no aim, no object, no sense, there *is* no time. One gives in, one surrenders, one's will is broken. All is prescribed, regulated, inevitable. All is senseless and hopeless, but one no longer realizes it. Only contrast and change create sensation, monotony kills it. Such monotony is a state very near death and very near that of Nirvana; it is the most unnatural state one can be in while still alive — but it is, to some natures at least, paradoxical as it may sound, a state as near complete happiness as one can obtain. But such happiness is for monks and nuns, and if you have ever been near it you will distinguish its reflection in their calm faces.

For that happiness is not for you in a prisoners' camp. You recognize its possibility, but you cannot approach it — for you are not alone. And that is the horror of horrors of that life, the one which not only does not lessen with time, but goes on increasing, and the one no one can imagine who has not been through it: *you are never alone*. Not by day, not by night, not for an hour, not for a second, day after day, year after year. During the war the term *maladie du fil de fer barbelé*, barbed wire sickness, became a recognized medical designation under which were grouped all sorts of mental symptoms observed in prisoners of war; but it is not the barbed wire which is their cause, it is the monstrous, enforced, incessant community which inevitably breeds the malady. There is nothing like it to be found anywhere else. Monks retire to their cells, soldiers have their days or weeks off; here it continues forever, and the longer it continues the more you suffer from it. No privacy, no possibility of being alone, no possibility of finding *quietude*. It is inhuman, cruel and dreadful to force people to live in closest community for years; it becomes almost unbearable when that community is abnormally composed like that of a prisoners' camp. There are no women, no children, there is no old age and next to no youth there, there is just a casual rabble of men forced to be inseparable. Try to imagine — though it is impossible really to understand without having experienced it — what it means, *never* to be *alone* and *never* to know *quiet*, not for a minute, and to continue thus for years, and you will begin to wonder that there was no general outbreak of insanity, that there yet remained a difference between lunacy and barbed wire nerves. The space allotted to a prisoner in a hut was exactly six feet by four (a coffin is six feet by two); besides that there was a space set aside for meals, etc., at the end of the hut, which just held the tables and necessary number of chairs. In your own 'space' you were as far removed from the next man as you can be in the hut, and that is a few feet. Nearly all people enclosed their space as time went on, converting it into a cubicle for one or possibly for more, but even then you naturally heard every sound through the thin matchboards which formed the partitions. You heard, in fact, every single noise in the hut, heard people talking, laughing, quarrelling, reading the paper aloud, practising the violin or some other instrument (often several at it at the same time); and they in their turn heard every word you spoke, every movement you made. And if you could have got used to the noise there was the vibration, which I found quite impossible ever to get accustomed to, for the floor consisted of thin, badly-joined boards laid on rafters, and whenever anyone walked in the hut or moved a chair it set up vibration right through the hut. At night you heard the breathing, snoring or whispering of thirty men (there is an incredible variety of such noises); some talked in their sleep, and every half (or was it quarter?) hour you heard the guards cry out to each other and your ears followed the sound right round the camp.

No one could stand staying in the hut for long; one soon developed a habit of rushing out every ten minutes or so. That habit became so much of a second nature that I found it very difficult to get rid of again in later years. One rushed round, one walked or ran round the camp a hundred times a day, one walked across it or between the huts by way of change, and wherever you went there were people just in front of you, just behind you, just beside you or just coming towards you, and they were always the same people. You could not talk to a friend without being overheard, you could not make a movement that was not watched. The control exercised by the prisoners over each other was infinitely more irritating and galling than the superficial outside control.

No one escaped the effects of such an existence. Its most inevitable results were of two kinds. There were the men who sank into an unlimited mutual intimacy based on mutual contempt. They lost all reserve, all sense of decency, they let themselves go altogether and gave up all that makes life in common tolerable to civilized men. They became what one calls beastly, though I don't know what beasts really behave in such a manner. I will say that there were not very many of these at Wakefield, from all accounts they must have formed the majority in the Knockaloe of the last years of war. The second effect produced by the conditions was far more general, in fact, I knew no one who escaped it altogether, and it can be described by the one word: *Hatred*. There was hatred of everyone against his neighbours, there was hatred of almost all against almost all. It is that atmosphere of irrational general hatred which is so astonishingly rendered in Dostoevsky's memories of *The House of the Dead*. People in all countries talked a great deal about their hatred of the enemy, but it was mostly talk, you cannot hate an abstraction; people with whom you do not come into contact are abstractions. In the same way the mechanically repeated professions of hatred against the British officers or guards or against the Government or the whole nation (as well as all the other allied nations, of course), was little more than a convention. Of course, the men felt bitter, but they did not hate; it was merely the same incredible pressure of what was supposed to be public opinion which forced people in England to express their hatred of anybody or anything German, and Germans their hatred of anybody or anything British which also affected the prisoners. Such hate I consider entirely unreal, for though it was purely accidental on which side a country fought in the end, it became automatically 'hated' by one side and 'loved' by the other when it had taken its stand, and it is a well-known fact that the soldiers of all nations who were almost the only people to come into contact with the enemy did very little hating indeed as compared to the violent pseudo-emotions of the people at home. The real reason of this universally professed hatred was, of course, that it made people feel that they were 'doing their bit' to help their country. A case I heard of while at Wakefield is a very good instance of how that hatred was constituted. A man there wished to leave the camp and work on a farm (in spite of the German Government's prohibition of such activities). He was married to an English girl, the daughter of a country squire, and she asked all the farmers on the estate whether they would take him. Each one said he would be only too pleased, workers being terribly scarce, of course, but he was forced to refuse. He himself did not mind having a German, particularly that German he knew very well, but he could not have him on account of the terrible hatred of all other farmers against the Germans. That is what each one said and what each one believed all the others' state of mind to be.

But if that sort of hatred was abstract, the hatred engendered inside the camp between its inmates was terribly concrete, was, indeed, inevitable. Every man almost is full of little foibles and more or less unpleasant mannerisms which his fellow creatures smile at or mildly object to in normal, everyday life. When human beings live together, as in married or family life, these easily lead to friction. It may be that such details play a far greater part in making married life unhappy than matters considered far more serious. In Flaubert's *Madame Bovary* Emma finally decides to murder her husband because she can no longer bear his nasty habit of drawing his last gulp of wine at dinner through his teeth by way of cleansing them. After my experiences in camp I consider this a stroke of genius, for of such a nature are the real causes of deadly hatred where humans are forced to live together and can see no end to that enforced mode of existence. Hundreds of such murders would have happened in camp had not fear of punishment prevented them. That may sound absurd, but human nature *is* absurd and it is quite irrational, and the worst tortures of camp life were due to small failings of one's fellow creatures everlastingly in evidence, and to unimportant little tricks endlessly repeated. It is not the men of bad character or morals you begin to hate, but the men who draw their soup through their teeth, clean their ears with their fingers at dinner, hiccough unavoidably when they get up from their meal (a moment awaited with trembling fury by the others), the men with ever dirty hands, the man who will invariably make the same remark (every day, year after year) as he sits down — and who is quite an inoffensive good-natured sort of creature otherwise — the man who lisps, the man who brags, the man who has no matter what small defect or habit you happen to object to. You go on objecting quietly, for one does not quarrel about such silly trifles, and the thing gets on your nerves, becomes unbearable by the simple process of endless repetition, until you hate the cause of your torture with a deadly hatred. Thus is created an atmosphere of mutual dislike, suspiciousness, meanness, hatred, which becomes almost tangible. Desperate quarrels break out for the most improbable motives, but these motives are only apparent and the real causes lie deeper and are subconscious. Men became deadly enemies over a piece of bread claimed by both; every suspicion of an unfair advantage due to protection of some sort, or of bribery, resulted in whole campaigns of slander, and bred new hatred between many. Such an atmosphere is thoroughly poisoned, all normal sense of proportion is lost, utterly unimportant matters assume gigantic size, and what is of real importance almost ceases to matter at all. That is what prison life of the nature here described leads people to and what it makes of them. It is not its privations, not its restrictions, not possible bad treatment by people in authority which are its worst features or its greatest dangers. Its true terror is that it has an indescribably degrading influence on the soul of man.

Chapter IX
Life in Wakefield

I have described what seems to me to have been the atmosphere of Wakefield and, indeed, of any prisoners' camp when one comes to look back at it after a number of years, when one is far enough from it to overlook the details and see the great outlines only. But, needless to say, I had no such clear and general conception of it after a few days there. I had realized I was a prisoner and I was very unhappy; I should say that the first few months at Wakefield were the worst of my whole captivity. Everything seemed just hopeless and futile and any effort senseless. If I ever was in danger of definitely 'giving in' it was then, but just at the beginning one could not sit still and await the end, for one had got to learn all about one's new surroundings, which differed a good deal from those one had got used to in the Isle of Man. They might be the same in their great outlines, but every trifling difference seems of great importance where there is so little possibility of variety.

Each day began, of course, by a parade, but here each hut was assembled and counted separately, and — an important privilege

— if it was wet one was counted inside the hut. Then one dressed, and that again was different, for one could wash in the hut if one bought the necessary implements, and most people did. Then came breakfast — and then came nothing. One walked round that square camp till one got sick of it; one walked round it so often that one developed a habit of automatically going off at a right angle after fifty yards or so. When I first regained freedom I found it quite an effort to keep on walking in the same direction for any greater distance. Dancing mice always remind me of Wakefield. Dinner was provided in the middle of the day, letters were distributed at four or five p.m., supper was at eight and lights out at ten. Those were the daily events. Twice a week one could write one of those empty letters and once a week one made out one's washing list. If letter writing and washing-list coincided, one felt, after some months of this regime, that too great a strain was being put on one, too much of an effort demanded of one's brain. There was nothing else one need do; one could idle all day, all the year. As, after all, no one forced one to eat or sleep, it might be said that all that was demanded of one was that one should put in an appearance twice daily in order to be counted.

One need do nothing, but doing nothing is possible only to very wise or to half-witted men, and even then only if they live in a warm climate, of in comfortable surroundings if in a cold country. So everyone almost did something and occupied himself in some manner. Time here really had to be *killed*, for it was the archenemy, and everyone tried to achieve this as best he could and according to his nature. The great thing was to try to forget the truth that no effort was worthwhile, that the work there could have no purpose, and as human nature is instinctively self-protective, whatever people did, soon became an end in itself. It was quite extraordinary what a manifold and complicated organization a prisoners' camp could become. The general mood underwent changes, of course; there were efforts and then disappointment with the results and realization of the futility of all efforts, and then renewed efforts after a period of gloomy idling. Only each new effort had less push and energy behind it, until in time they ceased altogether. My first months at Wakefield, however, were a period of great energy in the camp though they were one of deep depression to me personally. More particularly in our West Camp a good deal of energy was expended. When we had got there, it was a sandy waste and the interior of the huts as good as bare, but the people's ambition was aroused by comparison with what had been achieved in the two older camps. First of all they got busy with the grounds, built paths, planted shrubs, laid out a tennis court. The huts became places of separate 'rooms' containing furniture, curtains, books. One half of one hut was set aside for the musicians — of whom there were many — and housed a piano. When the Y.M.C.A. presented the camp with a large tent it was used as a reading room and a library was founded.

Soon we had lectures like the other camps had; everyone who thought he had something interesting to relate, or merely liked to hear himself speak, gave a lecture. One man who had lived many years in Russia lectured on conditions there; others knew all about the Dutch Indies, about the habits of migrating birds, or about the chemical industry in the U.S.A. It did not matter much at that time what a lecture was on or what it was worth, people were only too glad to while away an hour. Then people began teaching and learning, languages chiefly, but there were also courses in history and various branches of science. And after a year or so the camp became ambitious and decided, together with the two other camps, that Wakefield was the seat of a university! All the lectures, lessons, etc., were grouped into a sort of more or less coherent whole, and there were hundreds of students. Young men studied at this university with a view to their future and older men there were who had quite decided to change their profession and become men of learning. There was a half-hearted but loudly voiced belief that the German Government recognized Wakefield as an official seat of learning: men were not wasting their time there, the terms of studies would be counted, they would all receive degrees. It was a pathetic delusion.

Religious services there were for the different denominations, but religion played an astonishingly small part in the men's life. That is, I imagine, one aspect in which a German prisoners' camp in England must have differed a great deal from an English camp in Germany. I remember that on one occasion I wished to look up something in the Bible; I was unable to find a single copy of the Bible amongst all I knew and all they knew! We had art exhibitions, art consisting chiefly of inlaid woodwork which a number of people went in for; the things were very neatly executed and mostly quite atrocious. There were next to no artists among the prisoners. I know only of one portrait painter in the North Camp, and of one young fellow in the South Camp who did stage scenery and called himself an artist — besides myself. But musicians were plentiful, on the other hand, and of all varieties. There were a few very good professional musicians, a 'cellist, two violinists, one of whom was Hungarian while the second would be a Jugo-Slav nowadays; a very good pianist with a Polish name, all of whom gave recitals; there was a professional tenor who refused to appear in public, but had a pupil whom he allowed to perform. Amateur musicians were innumerable, from quite good to excruciatingly bad, and between them all they managed to form an orchestra which became quite creditable in time. It performed twice a week or so in the different camps, being one of the very few institutions which was common property of the three. Music was one of the saving graces of camp life, but, unfortunately, practising music was one of its worst drawbacks. Of the stage I shall have more to say presently; it was the only part of 'public life' I ever took a part in, though even that was on one or two occasions only.

In this I was one of a small minority, for nearly everyone seemed to have some sort of 'official position' he was proud of. It was a true *Beamtenstaat*[1]: everyone was administering and there was very little to administer; it was nearly all government and nothing much to be governed, and so really everyone administered the others by virtue of his office while being administered by them in their official capacities. I do not know whether this was characteristically German or whether the same phenomenon would be found in camps of different nationalities, but I think it was mainly due to the need for some sort of activity, for any activity in fact, of people unable to continue their real work in life and who felt they would go mad without some sort of occupation, the importance of which they grossly exaggerated in self-defence, for they could not have gone on with it if they had admitted the futility of their labours to themselves or to others.

So there were the captains and the chief-captains and their adjutants — very great men indeed, and as such exposed to the envy of the masses which often brought their downfall after a time. I remember the excitement in our camp when the first chief-captain there fell out of favour. He was, of course, accused of a *Schiebung*; I say 'of course,' because that was what invariably happened, but I don't remember any of the details. I do remember, though, that there was a conclave of the captains to talk the matter over which was interrupted by a man who had no business to be there at all, being quite an anonymous commoner and that he submitted the damning proofs to the assembly. They could not ignore them, but they were as furious about this breach of discipline as a council of field marshals interrupted by a private might have been. But the truly remarkable fact was that the great majority sided with them! They did not deny that that man's intervention had served the cause of all, but they did not think

---

[1] German: Bureaucratic state.

that justified his undisciplinary interference. Really a surprising state of mind it seemed to me, but very few shared my surprise. After some years of experience of mass psychology in camp I am of opinion that the average man's desire for liberty is very much smaller than is generally supposed or argued. He hates and fears responsibility far more than he desires independence; what he really likes is sharing some of the power without taking any risks and delegating responsibility to ever higher grades of officialdom until it vanishes in thin air on the highest mountain top. He likes to grouse and to talk about how much better things would be done if he had the power to manage them, but he does not really desire that power. And that is why he gets furious when some people not content with grousing actively attack superior and sheltering authorities.

Complaints about corruption and improper use of office against the officials never stopped, and people were incredibly suspicious. There were, of course, lots of opportunities for dishonesty connected with the buying of provisions, coal, etc., for the camp; some very bad cases were proved, but control was difficult and mostly the truth about the case remained doubtful. But no matter how bad the case might be — and there were some very bad ones in connection with kitchen and hospital arrangements — the fury of the camp was only directed against the guilty individual, never against the authorities as such. I think that the success of dictatorships of varying kinds in so many European countries at the present time shows that such psychology is by no means limited to prisoners' camps, but very much more universal than an optimistic pre-war intelligentsia supposed.

Some of the less important officials (lesser in grade, for their functions were really much more useful) were employed in the post offices where the fate of letters and parcels depended on them, as far as the military authorities did not interfere, and as rulers of the kitchen realm. There we possessed some eminent specialists and their position was tragi-comic. Quite an astounding number of the chefs of the first London hotels must have been German or Austrian before the war, though the innocent public, of which I formed part, had always been led to believe that the chefs of all first-class hotels of the world were French. Well, here we had the kitchen-kings of many world-famous hotels and restaurants set to the task of making the best of horseflesh, antique herrings, or frozen potatoes, combined with margarine. Next there were those connected with the hospital, and the great number of heads or members of committees of all sorts. I have already mentioned the 'university' where a real university professor of history did much directing; there was also a professional philosopher (unprofessional ones were fairly frequent), and the teachers of Turkish, Russian, and many other languages. As there was an orchestra, there were conductors, members of the orchestra, and, of course, a music subcommittee of the entertainment committee; as there were two theatres, there were directors, actors, and stage workers of different sorts. There were the leaders of sport, for a good many games were practised. Tennis flourished exceedingly; for the camp boasted the two leading German professionals of the time, Froitzheim and Kreutzer, who had been playing in Australia when war broke out. There was an annual tournament, and their exhibition match was one of the very great events of the year. All the British officers put in an appearance: royalty, if a very unpopular royalty, was present! Hockey as well was played in the North Camp, where there was sufficient space, and boxing was taught by a Turkish professional, Sabri Mahir, who was the organizer of the first boxing matches in Berlin after the war, which were also the first ever seen in Germany. There were some doctors and dentists — not official, for one was supposed to go to the hospital only for treatment, and at the hospital there were the nurses. Last, but by no means least, there were the men who really plied their trade, and they were all too few in numbers: tailors, cobblers, barbers, stewards. As there were only fifteen hundred men all told that really left but a small minority without some form of 'employment.' Of these a certain number pursued some aim of their own, and the remnant really did nothing except play cards or drink when they got the chance. Their number was not very considerable and it was unequally divided between the three camps, the West Camp having few indeed and the South Camp most.

It may appear as if that account of universal activity contradicts my earlier statement about the unending monotony of camp life, but the contradiction is more apparent than real. First of all because the men's occupations, such as I have defined them, only took up a very small part of the day, but more yet because all that activity was artificial and most men were aware of this. With very few exceptions they were doing some sort of work that would lead them nowhere, as they well knew. They were continually giving it up and taking it on again in despair, simply because they could not face entirely empty days. So most of them were working at something, but at something which was not in their line at all really, and which they did not care about in the least, for the consciousness of the futility of their work never left them, and that sense of futility caused a sensation of unending monotony, of dead calm even when there was outward movement. The main cause of dissatisfaction with one's work and of the impossibility of concentrated and deliberate efforts was, I think, the fact that one knew no limit to the time one would have to spend there. After the first year of war was over one felt desperate as the second winter approached, and after that there seemed no possibility of the war ever ending at all. Nor did one know whether one would not be suddenly transferred to some other camp, and such rumours were ever rife. Everything was uncertain and precarious; it might be worthwhile to plant seeds for the following spring or it might be a waste of energy, one might reap benefits from one's studies when release came, but that release might come too late or never.

Any definite term of imprisonment would have been better than that uncertainty which made all plans and movements in any direction appear senseless.

But this people only admitted to themselves in moments of utter despondency. They went on as if they knew where they were going to. Young men and old studied at the university, eager to get on, but the young men would have to re-become bank clerks and the old men have to try to earn their living. Such well-thought-out plans there were! A man I knew was desperately trying to master Turkish and Arabic, because the Germans would hold Palestine and own the Baghdad railway and develop half Asia. One of his uncles was a commander there, so he must know, and he persevered in his faith until the end. The enthusiasm of the actors was surprising, but most surprising that of the men who specialized in female parts. Where could it all lead to? But the truth was, that the future was an absolute blank and that the present had to be got over somehow. Without illusions about the importance of their doings and about the future most would have gone mad. And this senseless and useless waste of energy is one of the many dark sides of the internment of civilians.

The people who suffered least in that particular way were undoubtedly the stewards (mostly ex-waiters), barbers, and tailors who were the only ones to continue to exercise their professions. In this gentlemen's camp the lot of that small minority not counted amongst them was privileged in more ways than one. Here as in Knockaloe the law of supply and demand held true, but as here the Government allowed only a strict minimum of such non-paying prisoners, conditions were the exact reverse from those obtaining in the Isle of Man. There hundreds had run after work; here the few qualified workers were run after by the 'capitalist class.' As a result they were generally very high and mighty indeed, regarded their services as favours conferred, and were very expensive. This did not tend to make life pleasanter for the majority, which is perhaps where social justice came in for once; but for that ungentlemanly minority Wakefield was really a privileged camp. In the last two years, however, matters changed somewhat, for a growing number of prisoners had to find paid work in the camp if they wished to continue paying their ten shillings a week. So they ceased to be gentlemen in order to continue to be gentlemen in the eyes of the law, stewards became plentiful, even private stewards made an appearance, and the social order was restored to a more normal balance.

Chapter X
Three Camps

Officially there was but one prisoners' camp at Lofthouse Park, Wakefield, but it had been divided into three parts. While the Knockaloe 'compounds' each held one thousand men, each of these 'camps' only held five hundred, and I have never understood the reasons of this sub-division. I suppose it just happened, or else the authorities thought it simpler to add new camps rather than increase the original one when that became too small. I suppose they had not counted on finding so many 'gentlemen' amongst their prisoners. Whatever the cause may have been, the division was a fact and a very unpleasant one. To begin with, it restricted the space one could move in, which would have been none too great even if the three camps had formed one. It also restricted the possibilities of human intercourse by mainly limiting one to the men in one's own camp. For having once decided that three camps were preferable to one, everything was done to keep them separate, and this was most unnecessarily irritating. All three together were, of course, enclosed by barbed wire and guarded, so that there was no imaginable risk in allowing the men to move all over the place, but that idea did not please officialdom and so even such modest freedom of movement was never granted. If one wished to visit one of the other camps one had to apply for a pass the day beforehand, and it had to be signed by the second officer in command, who might refuse to do so if he thought the number of passes granted too great. If there was a performance in one camp, a general pass was issued to members of the other camps, but here again the number of men allowed to cross the borders was strictly limited. And stopping all passes was a favourite form of punishment for some minor offences committed. Having obtained a pass, one handed it to a soldier who liked to make one wait before unlocking the gate, after which one was free of that other barbed wire partition, but only during the hours set aside for such delirious joys. They ended at six p.m. if I remember right. Some very privileged people obtained weekly or even monthly passes, but I was never one of the lucky, and never learnt the secret subterfuges by which such favours were obtained. Everything has its two sides, however, and as a visit to another camp was not so easy it became quite an adventure, a change one looked forward to, just as visiting another hut in one's own camp would have seemed a privilege if it had only been allowed on exceptional occasions. I recommend such a system to all would-be tyrants: begin by making laws and conditions as severe as possible and relax them a very little gradually or on certain occasions, and you will find many to bless your name and but few to see through you.

The three camps were very instructive in many ways. For one thing, one learnt the huge importance of frontiers, the results of division. The frontiers here were but of barbed wire, but that was quite enough to make people learn to consider the inmates of one of the other camps as strangers and as questionable as all strangers are. One got, in fact, an extraordinary opportunity of studying the rise and growth of nationalism. Here there were no different races, languages, religion, or historical origins, but as there was an artificial division there was a feeling of separate entities, of difference, of strangeness as between neighbouring peoples. Individual friendships and good personal relations were very frequent, which is not unusual between people of different nationality either in normal times, but 'the camp' existed above and separately from the men who composed it; it was a state, a nation to which one belonged while those of another camp did not — they were outsiders. Human nature would not be what it is if things had stopped there, and they did not. People outside barbed wire prefer their country to others, so do people inside the wire, in short, 'patriotism' of sorts arose and led to rivalry. I have read much about friendly rivalry amongst nations, but so far I have failed to find any; on the other hand, I have seen more than enough hostile rivalry, nor do I find that it has got any the less after the war which was caused by it. The different parts of the old Austrian empire got on none too well with each other, but that is nothing compared to their mutual hostility since they are divided by frontiers and free to compete with each other in armaments and trade. In the same way the barbed wire divisions created hostility, distrust and dislike, which went on increasing as the years passed by. I don't think a rupture of mutual relations would have been out of the question if more years had passed. As it was, there were all the absurdities of nationalism: you must prefer your own 'country' to the others, you must not profess too much approval of their institutions or characteristics, you must stand up for your 'own people' against 'the strangers.' Things had not developed as far as active hostility, they were in the stage of more or less polite disdain; each camp was convinced of its own superiority, and if it could not deny that the other camp possessed certain advantages — well, they were not advantages they themselves would have cared for. If it would be too much to say that they disliked each other as the French might the Germans or the Turks the Greeks, their attitude to each other might be compared to that of Prussians, Bavarians, and Austrians who, while united as against the foreigner, cordially disliked and despised each other, and would insist not on their obvious common characteristics but on their more or less trifling differences.

As between peoples, it is ever difficult to decide whether there is a primary difference between them which finds its expressions in frontiers and divisions, or whether it is the divisions which are the cause of the differences, though it is quite certain that divisions must accentuate differences. But in Wakefield the case was quite clear and therefore all the more instructive: there was no difference whatsoever between the men of one camp or the other, but the division created a conviction of essential difference and in time differences actually came to exist. Each camp became slightly distinct in character from the others, the difference would have, I imagine, been invisible and incomprehensible to an outsider, but it was a reality to the people concerned.

It is so terribly easy to create divisions, so terribly difficult to bridge them over when once created. There is difference everywhere, quite insignificant as compared to essential similarity, but most easily enhanced. English and French are extremely alike when compared, let us say, with the aborigines of darkest Africa, but how essentially different a Breton feels from a Marseillais, a Highlander from a Cockney! So all depends on the point of view. One may state that all human beings are extremely alike when compared to fish or birds, or that not two members of one family are really alike. Both statements are true, but it is equally true that to insist on differences is not conducive to peace. So it is true in a sense that there were differences between the type of men who formed one camp or the other; they had not — taken *en masse* — exactly the same antecedents (just as little as any two individuals would have), but if there had been but one camp these differences would have merged into an entity. As there were three, they inevitably started to accentuate them.

The majority of the men in each camp bore no very marked character, they were just that crowd which always takes its cue from some leader or leaders; it was that minority of leaders which differed from one camp to the other and which in time stamped each with a character of its own.

The South Camp was the oldest of the three, and in every way the least conventional. I have already alluded to its central hall, and that rather dilapidated reminder of past frivolity was not only its centre but also a kind of symbol. There was nothing military-looking in that rather untidy agglomeration; some huts were larger, some smaller, and they looked as if they had been dumped down anywhere where there happened to be room. The hospital lay at one end, and at the other there was a tiny copse where in summer people actually lay on the ground instead of in gentlemanly and proper deckchairs. The dominant note of the South Camp was colonial. There were a good many men from the German colonies in Africa, and riding-breeches and wide-brimmed hats were in evidence. There was certainly a good deal of drinking and possibly — the rumour was persistent — not a little drug-taking. Many of the people had lived in tropical climates, many had had adventurous voyages before they were taken off some ship by the British, some looked rather desperate. All had been interned for a good long time already, and most of them had very little money. There was an untidy, furtive and rather romantic atmosphere in that camp. Few of the men had friends outside their own camp and most of them seemed to have few friends inside it, but to keep to themselves. They had made next to no improvements in their camp, there were no sports; there seemed little social life of any sort with the exception of theatricals. Probably there were quite a number of original characters to be found there, but they avoided strangers and one did not come across them. When in 1917 the erection of tiny single huts was permitted, a few wealthy men moved to the South Camp where there was room to build them;

there was the director of a well-known bank, there was some sort of dignitary from Turkey, but they, too, seemed to lead solitary lives. The South Camp was inclined to be cranky, the other camps shrugged their shoulders at it, while their *bourgeois* neatness was despised by the South. In that strange and abnormal camp-city this was 'Bohemia.'

The North Camp was frigid and correct as its name suggests. Its huts stood on flat, featureless ground, all similar, symmetrically disposed, monotonous and depressing. A largish waste space served for games: there were tennis courts, there was a corrugated iron hall, very ugly, but neat and clean inside, which had a stage and many chairs of yellow wood. The whole place looked well-kept and extremely dreary. It was, I suppose, a model prisoners' camp. Also it was doubtlessly socially superior. There were few men there who had lived in England; they had mostly lived somewhere abroad and a good many had been 'captured' at Gibraltar; the majority were young men. Many were of the Hanseatic type, in its way one of the best German types, though not a very exhilarating one; they were well-mannered, correct, cool and slow. There were a number of former officers or reserve officers; I think the two tennis champions belonged to that class. And last but not least there were a number of titled men to enhance the camp's social glory. It must be remembered that in pre-war Germany the nobility, *der Adel*,[1] lived a life socially separated from the other classes, hardly mixing with anyone outside its rank. So it was perhaps natural that in camp as well they congregated and that there was one hut which went by the name of *die Grafenhütte*[2] because a number of the counts, barons, etc., had elected it for their common residence. I say 'perhaps' because some of the nicest of the nobles could not stand its feudal atmosphere and preferred to live anywhere

---

1 German: The eagles: i.e., the elite of the camp.

2 German: The hut of the *Graffen* (Counts).

else. But it was that hut which impressed popular imagination and which was responsible for what the North Camp stood for in the eyes of the other camps and in its own to a great extent. Its inmates regarded it with a mixture of awe and distrust, but they were proud of it, while the other camps felt envy and dislike, and declared, of course, that they would never have put up with that crying scandal of social inequality in a place where all were comrades in misfortune.

The North Camp was very Prussian and prided itself on being much more severely national than the others (which did not allow this claim for a minute). If it had been English, it would have been very representative of the 'public school spirit'; as it was, it was representative of the spirit of that class of Germans which corresponds as nearly as possible to the public school class in England. Opinions, political opinions particularly, were strictly orthodox and prescribed, bad manners were discouraged, dress was conventional. There were social strata which kept apart from each other, and relations were rather formal. There were certainly a good many rebels against these conventions, but so there are in public schools, without affecting their general character. The North Camp maintained a certain standard of behaviour of which it had reason to be proud, but it was also very inclined to snobbishness. It was the 'Mayfair' (a pre-war Mayfair) of the camp-city. Consciously or unconsciously, its inhabitants tried to live up to the standards of the aristocrats in their midst, though they would have disputed this just as furiously as do all imitators of aristocracy, at liberty or caged. And the joke of the situation is similar in both cases, for the only people who do not believe in these standards, or think them useful perhaps, but a bore, are the very aristocrats — amongst whom are to be found the only ones not to be snobs. So in the North Camp the least conventional, the least nationalist and narrow-minded, and the ones who cared least about social standing, were a number — the majority indeed — of the counts, barons, and *freiherren*.[3] And, again, as in normal, life, they could not give the show away.

My own camp, the West, had the least character and was the most colourless and monotonous of the three. It was anything but romantically slipshod, and it could not claim much social standing. It was essentially middle-class. Nearly all its inmates were businessmen who had lived in England before the war; a very few in a big way of business, but mostly men of moderate means. There was a majority of middle-aged, a minority of young men, mostly city clerks. Though it seemed to me that they were much of a muchness, that was evidently due to my ignorance, for there were plenty of recognized social distinctions. On the very first day I had learnt to my great surprise that bank clerks possessed high social value and were superior to clerks in any other business. The *Bankbeamtenhütte*[4] was pointed out to me, and I found that it was to the West what the *Grafenhütte* was to the North. In fact, the inmates of that hut had strong 'northern' tendencies and more friends in that camp than in their own. Besides the sacred legion of bank clerks, some even more socially eminent dwelt there: a director of an important industrial concern (who was a sort of uncrowned king of the camp) and a professor. There was not very much to choose between the other huts, but that did not prevent them from a good deal of mutual despising. To the other camps they were all suspect, socially they were quite undistinguished, and they were besides suspected of lukewarm patriotism. This made them shout all the louder, of course, but to no avail. As a matter of fact, their position was rather different from that of the majority of the other camps. The elder men in particular had had their business in England which obviously they did not wish to see ruined;

---

3 German: Free Lord, a title in German nobility ranked just below *Graf* (Count).

4 German: Bank clerks' hut.

many had their families living in that country even then, and they must in their interest wish to pass for as little hostile as possible, and some had English wives and possibly naturalized children. All their interests in the past lay in England and they might lie there again in the future. This was a very different position from that of men who had never lived in England, never been near the place in many cases, and who looked on it simply as a country which was the enemy of their own and kept them prisoners. Their case was clear and simple, that of the others ambiguous and open to doubts, so in spite of all protests they were looked on as animals of a different and inferior species. The West held other elements as well which were considered not above suspicion, a good many Austrians and Hungarians and a good many Jews; and, needless to say, anti-semitism was by no means unknown, though on the whole in its politely disguised form.

The West Camp did its best in spite of these inborn weaknesses, but there was not much it could do to distinguish itself. Its only glory were the musicians (mostly Hungarian, Austrian, or Jewish) and that was all right as far as it went. But where the others had halls of great splendour, the West only possessed a very inferior and rather small Y.M.C.A. hut; the virtuosi desired the largest possible audience (at one shilling or one and a half) and so nearly all concerts were held in the North Camp which thus took to itself even that one outstanding merit. There was no stage, only a tiny platform, so there were no theatricals to attract 'foreign visitors'; there was no sports ground, and if there was one tennis court, the North Camp had several and its famous champions as well. I am afraid it must be admitted that there was very little to boast about in the West Camp or to recommend it to others. It was very drab and featureless, it was suburban. Its inmates might in moments of pride look on it as a Hampstead (whence, by the way, a good many hailed), but the others looked on it as Mayfair and Chelsea look on Peckham Rye. Had they all three been merged into one — let us say Kensington — they would have got on quite well together and intermingled to a very great extent. There would have been no more than the normal and, as it would seem, incurable desire of human beings to form groups on the principle of excluding others for some reason or other, but there would have been no large unfriendly wholes. Life would have been more varied, freedom of movement and choice of intercourse less restricted, mental and physical health better. But somewhere there was someone or several someones who decided some day for some reason — or possibly no reason: better have three separate camps. And that settled that.

Chapter XI
Some Men and their Stories

When I think back and try to recall my fellow prisoners of three years at Wakefield I see a grey, anonymous mass from which gradually emerge the figures of those with whom I came into closer personal contact and others distinguished by some degree of originality. Of these last there were far fewer than there had been in Knockaloe. At Wakefield the men were mainly of one class; class distinctions there were minute enough to be unreal, they were artificially created; Wakefield was almost entirely *bourgeois*, and whatever the good qualities of the *bourgeois* may be, originality or picturesqueness is emphatically not amongst them. Most interesting characters of Knockaloe had belonged to 'the people' and that was only present in very reduced numbers at Wakefield. I cannot say that any member of it I knew was in any way out of the ordinary, and I doubt if I would recognize the face of any one of the stewards, barbers, etc., which it consisted of. Maybe that is due to the fact that at Wakefield they had again become a distinct class: wage-earners in the service of employers, and that therefore one got to know them no better than one would have done in everyday life. They were as a rule thoroughly convinced of their (very real) indispensability and anything but pleasant. There probably were some amongst the colonials who would have been worth knowing, but they belonged to the distant and disdainful South and I never met them. Our own camp had but a few pseudo-exotics, men who bore Spanish or Dutch names because they had tried to reach Germany with false passports. They had been discovered and imprisoned, but they naturally stuck to their fiction. I felt a good deal of sympathy for all those who had been arrested on ships after a long voyage, amongst other reasons probably because I am a very bad sailor. The worst case I heard of was that of two Austrian officers who arrived one day — God knows why — in our civilian midst. They had escaped, after years of imprisonment and under the greatest hardships, from Siberia and reached a Chinese port. There they had procured themselves false passports and taken service as stewards on a neutral steamer. They voyaged round half the world, passed ever so many ports under British control, and were finally fetched off their boat at the first English port by smiling and courteous military officials and imprisoned once more! That was the British system, and I heard of many such cases; the British authorities at all ports were perfectly aware of the identity of such people, but they let them pass unhindered until they reached England or the nearest controlled port on their route. Meanwhile these men had gone through all the agonies of fear of detection repeatedly and were all the more furious to discover at the end that they had been tricked all the time. A real cat and mouse game it was. Such had been the fate of, for instance, Mr. Müller of Java, who was not as Dutch as his papers. He had journeyed thence via the controls of Singapore, Colombo, Aden, until Port Said, where the British thought he'd better come off. Fortunately for him, he was of a cheerful disposition, stout, rubicund, fair-bearded, and content to drown his sorrows; but I remember another Mephistophelian man who never ceased to tremble with rage, and with malaria, poor thing. Besides these, far-travelled but Teutonic, there were a few of genuine foreign extraction: Turkish subjects. Besides Sabri the boxer, already mentioned, there were two Turkish Jews, uncle and nephew. Both were very handsome, of the real flashy Levantine breed so frequent in Paris. They were released after some months in a very remarkable manner. Like all the Jews of Salonika, they had come there from Spain at the time of the Inquisition and all these people's language is to this day Spanish, a Spanish of the fifteenth or sixteenth century. Heaven knows how it was all managed, but they were set free at the instigation of the Spanish ambassador — surely the first case in which the Spanish Government has claimed such infidels as subjects! I felt rather sore about this, for being of the same extraction I should have received the same treatment, but no Spanish grandee came to my rescue.

Amongst the Hungarians there were two very good professional violinists and one very strange young man, tall, dark, and very quiet, who also played a good deal. He shut himself off from people more and more as time passed by and would hardly answer when spoken to. And then a day came when he was removed to the hospital in a great hurry, religious mania suddenly burst through his enforced calm; he was, he declared, Jesus Christ and would therefore tear off all his clothes. He was taken away from the hospital a few hours later, and that was the last I ever heard or saw of him.

There were some pleasant figures amongst the actors. A Viennese youth in our camp was the leading lady of society comedies or dramas; he is one of the few I have met again later in life, when I found him holding a high position in a bank in Vienna and married to an extremely pretty woman who looked not at all unlike him in some of his great stage-parts, which he then did not seem to care to be reminded of. Some of the best actors were former army officers. There was one captain, born to be an aide-de-camp or gentleman-at-arms, so distinguished and full of tact was he. And all parts of similar character he played to perfection. When I last heard of him he was a *maître de plaisir*[1] at an aristocratic German spa, a most suitable post for him, and very popular in that capacity. Another man who had been a lieutenant and bore a well-known military name, appeared almost like one of the caricatures of the stiff, brainless, monocled, and haw-hawing Prussian lieutenants to be found in the German comic papers of pre-war times, but he turned out to be a quite astonishingly gifted actor, equally at ease in comic and in serious parts. Of all the amateurs there he was the only one who ought to have become a professional actor and who would have made a success of it; I heard, however, that he got himself mixed up with one of the new semi-military organizations, though one was not quite certain of this.

There was a good deal of variety among the small but select crowd of 'Northern nobles' and I don't think any one of them was quite dull, probably because they had seen a good deal of the world and were, in many cases, of cosmopolitan parentage. Some few were very wealthy, the others had had to earn their livings and amongst these a number had chosen curious professions. One Prussian grandee had been jiu-jitsu instructor to the London Police for instance, and was a most remarkable looking man with a fantastically shaped nose very like that adopted by actors in the part of Cyrano de Bergerac; he was quite unassuming and had charming manners. That might indeed have been said about most of them, though there were a few notable exceptions, but they passed for conceited and standoffish all the same. The majority of the others could not look on them or treat them as similar and ordinary human beings; they stood in awe of them or loathed them, admired or despised them for what they were supposed to be, without regard to what they really were. And really

---

1 French: Master of ceremonies.

they differed a good deal amongst themselves. One was very much an adventurer of the type one might meet at the Monte Carlo of pre-war times, and as he was none too sure of himself, he was aggressive and disdainful; but he was rather an amusing character really, with a slight whiff of the race-course and the gambling den about him. Another, elder man, who had, I believe, been in the diplomatic service, had spent many years in China. He had become a connoisseur of Chinese art and a fervent admirer of the culture and refinement of the Mandarins; he was a bon vivant and a gourmet and had learned a good deal of Eastern cunning. Of course, he loathed the camp and what he considered the barbaric denseness of its inhabitants, but his sentiments were hidden behind a mask of cordial joviality and he was far more popular than any of his peers. In the first afterwar years he established himself as a *marchand-amateur.* (a tactful and untranslatable French term) of Chinese works of art, and did very well, I believe. By this time he may have returned to his 'spiritual home.' There were others who did not possess his diplomatic gifts; one in particular, very well born and related to all sorts of royalty, was a very difficult customer. People in the camp he just ignored, with a very few exceptions, but he was always having terrific rows with the military authorities; he seemed to be in a continuous state of overwrought excitement, and was certainly one of those who suffered most from his condition and environment. He was and is still, I suppose, a big landowner and very rich. One of his very few friends was much of the same type, only his was the frigid variety. He had been a governor or some such thing in an African colony, was married to an Englishwoman and would have been quite in his proper atmosphere in the most conservative of clubs around St. James's. Always perfectly dressed, he held himself very straight and seemed frozen and unbending. Whether he was what he seemed I cannot say, for he was one of the few I never got to know. To their group might be added one rather pathetic elderly man who lived in the West Camp. I suppose he cannot have been above fifty, as he was interned, but he seemed more like seventy with his grey beard and trembling hands. He had lived many years in England and married an Englishwoman, and he was of the type which would be respected and highly considered at Bournemouth or Cheltenham. He was fidgety and finikin,[2] and camp life was to him a continuous series of shocks. The West Camp shocked him beyond endurance and he left it after what he considered a dreadful scandal. There was a man in his hut in every way his opposite and who could not bear him. He was a doctor of philosophy, and his chief interest was literature. He was a wild, shaggy and bushy-looking creature, something between Francois Villon and a youngish Bernard Shaw. Needless to say, he was considered a wild eccentric and was extremely unpopular. What happened was that he appeared one night before the unfortunate aged grand-seigneur entirely naked, shook him roughly by the shoulder and shouted at him: 'Kneel and adore the beauty of the body masculine!' It must have been quite a hideous sight, at any rate it was too much for his victim, who quite failed to see the humorous side of the incident. He complained bitterly, there was quite a row, and he left the West for the North, and, as he explained with tremulous dignity, the company of his peers. I hope they managed to avoid wounding his susceptibilities, but I am afraid they thought him a frightful old bore.

Several of my personal friends were members of the band of the chosen few, but they had all broken away from it to lead an independent existence in non-courtly and unsung huts or even inferior camps. I would like to say that this is a species of humanity I have always found very attractive and consider very valuable to a country and to society. Aristocrats have certain advantages which it is absurd to deny; they have lived in material ease

---

2 Excessively fastidious.

for generations, received good education, occupied a privileged position and had better opportunities all the way round for centuries — in fact, they have breeding, which is no less important in human animals than in others and achieves similar results. A certain number of pure-blooded ancestors are a great advantage; too many mostly result in decadence. There is such a thing as a hereditarily acquired faculty of leadership beside that belonging to exceptional personalities. On the other hand, as is well-known, mongrels are usually more intelligent than pedigree animals, every medal having its reverse. If the aristocracy (in the true sense of the word) should have the advantage in physique and in character, great intelligence is not one of its usual attributes. But if an aristocrat possesses intelligence as well as his usual qualities he becomes a very valuable specimen of humanity, and one of the signs of this is that he becomes bored with the class he belongs to and branches out in some other direction. He seeks to add to himself what he has not got, which is the sign of all superior men, whereas the average continue in the condition they were born in, and fear, dislike, or despise what is outside their native environment. The men of surpassing value are those who rise to lead, but also those who descend (in the social sense) to lead, because only that 'descension,' not condescension, can give them the contact with the majority or the masses every true leader in any field of activity needs. They are the type of people who make the 'revolution from above,' the Mirabeaus and Tolstoys of this world.

My friends there were not Mirabeaus and Tolstoys, but they were very much less narrow-minded than most others, and much more inclined to take an interest in more general matters and things outside the everyday life of the camp and the chances of the war. If they were alike as far as birth went, they were very different in education and outlook on life. Count E.'s father had been a general and he himself an officer in a guard regiment attached to one of the larger courts of Southern Germany. His family was a very ancient

Rhenish one, but his branch was not very wealthy, so that an army career seemed the very thing for him. But he took a violent dislike to all that is military and found life at court exceedingly boring, so he had left the army a year or so before the war and gone to the U.S.A. He had hated New York, except its east side, and moved on to Florida where he was growing oranges when war broke out. He returned to Germany and got as far as Gibraltar whence he came to Wakefield. He was a cheerful young man, but as he hated stuck-up people on one side and vulgarians on the other he made but few friends. He was very fond of music, and his mother who knew this advised him to hire a piano if his 'cubicle' would hold one. His answer to this got him into trouble with the authorities, for he wrote: 'No, my cubicle will not hold a piano, but a piano would more than hold my cubicle.' Camp life got on his nerves badly, he lost his cheerfulness and became wrapped up in mysticism, and after a time a convinced Rosicrucian. He made himself a picture of the cross wreathed with roses on a golden background and hung it over his bed. His very worldly original nature and this contemplative mysticism formed the oddest contrast, but he seemed much more satisfied than before. I don't think he ever quite recovered his equilibrium. After the war he found himself very poor, tried all sorts of trades, married to get divorced again after a very short time, and never seemed to know where he belonged. The Baron H. was one of his very few friends and he introduced me to him. H. had been educated in a cadet-school and been a naval officer. I forget whether he had already left that service before the war or whether he had only meant to, but he had married a girl he blindly adored and who was disapproved of by the Service as she was considered of too low an extraction. There were, of course, all sorts of rules and regulations as to whom officers might or might not marry. He was a tall, emaciated, very fair man, very delicate, and in a very bad state of health. He had one fixed idea which was to return to his wife, and this influenced his health. If he were ill enough, he would be sent back, and no one could tell how far he really was ill, how far he wished to appear so, or how far his desire for sickness had become actually effective. At any rate, he walked with difficulty and the aid of a stick, looked like a ghost, and his nerves were overstrung to breaking point. Apart from that he had exquisite manners, was very shy and retiring, of almost feminine sensitiveness, very fond of poetry, very well read, and rather sentimental. He never achieved his wish and he got more and more strange. He became convinced of his power, furthered by fasting and prayer (for he was also very religious) to enter into spiritual communication with his wife. These efforts quite exhausted him, but he was almost happy after he had found that apparent solution to his great trouble. The end of the war should have brought perfect happiness and peace to him at least, but things turned out very differently indeed. When he got back, he found that while he had held spirit-intercourse with his wife she had held very physical intercourse indeed with other men. He left her, and next I heard that he had eloped with the wife of a friend of his. He did not marry her, however: they quarrelled, and he accused her of having tried to induce him to poison his uncle, from whom he was to inherit a great fortune. Next I heard — for I never saw him again — that he had married a Japanese, then that his uncle had died — some people said under curious circumstances, and last — that he had poisoned his wife and children, set his castle on fire and shot himself. They managed to save the wife's life, but he and the children died. His was one of the very many camp tragedies I have known which reached their climax years after the war. None of the men I knew personally went mad or killed themselves while imprisoned, but a number of them did in the years following their release: they had survived the adaptation to camp life but they had not enough strength left for the second and quite as difficult adaptation to normal existence. None of these catastrophes was due to material difficulties.

If I should have prophesied calm happiness in store for the Baron H., I should have predicted a most venturesome future to the Freiherr von K. But there again I may have been wrong, only I have not the slightest notion of what has become of that entertaining youth. He was quite a boy, nineteen, I believe, and had an elder brother in another camp whom he hardly ever saw. They had nothing to say to each other, the elder being a quiet, ordinary person, and the younger very much of a Bohemian. Their father had been an officer and belonged to a famous family, some of whom had come over to England with George I. Perhaps that had attracted him to England; anyway, he had come to live there and married the daughter of his landlady or, at any rate, someone of that description. They seem to have had very little money, lived in Brixton or thereabouts, and apparently let their children grow up quite wild. They either went to some local board-school or else to no school at all, and I don't believe the parents had ever troubled about them in afterlife. The elder went into some sort of office and settled down, but the younger remained wild. He was a very curious sort of boy, as might, indeed, have been expected. He had decided to become a painter, but as he never had the money for a regular training he had worked as an aid to a stage scene painter and lived on God knows what expedients. He was a picturesque figure, tall and lanky with long hair untidily overhanging his brow and clothes either too large or too small for him, generally covered with stains of many colours. He was quite uneducated naturally, had lived his life in various slums, spoke English with a Cockney accent and no German at all until he learnt a little in camp. I don't know how he ever got there, for he certainly was not a gentleman according to the ten-shilling standard; it is doubtful whether many people would have considered him one according to the more usual standards. His 'peers,' at any rate, avoided him, but he avoided them at least as anxiously, and the language he used with regard to them was very spicy. He lived in the South

Camp, the only one where he could have existed at all, and if he had any friends they were stewards or colonials, but I don't think he was friends with anybody much. He didn't care a hang what others thought about him and called them all 'a lot of stinking skunks.' His language was very dirty and so was he, but that did not prevent him from having what the French call *très grand air* with his small, well-shaped head, defiant eyes, rather regal nose, and long, thin, perfectly shaped, and extremely unwashed hands. He worked quite hard — which very few people did — for he did all the stage scenery for his camp and painted a good many pictures besides. These were bought by the colonials and painted to their order: negro girls in a state of great undress in flamboyantly tropical scenery. They and other fantasies he did for his own pleasure would certainly have been unanimously refused by all the academies of the world, but just as he had unmistakable traces of the grand seigneur under a slum covering, so his pictures had traces of real genius under their slapdash clumsiness. In fact, the whole boy was a crying example of tragic waste, and his moodiness was due to the fact that he sometimes dimly realized this. Mostly, however, he got drunk in his spare time or played cards. There was some row about drugs in the South Camp, which was kept very dark by all concerned and by the authorities, and he was supposed to be the chief culprit. He grinned when I asked him about this and did not deny it, but he would tell me nothing about it. We were quite good friends though; he came to see me sometimes and shook his head over my drawings, but he always asked me to come round and criticize his own works of art which was by no means easy. Rarely have I met anyone so utterly lonely and without roots in family, class, or country. I suppose he was sent to Germany after the war (I never understood why he was not considered a British subject, having been born in England), but, if so, he did not stay there, for some years ago a friend of mine came across him in New York. He was then a step-dancer in a fifth-rate cabaret.

No stronger contrast to him could have been found than my friend J. He too was a baron and of a family which bore a historic name and was related to similar families all over Europe, but particularly in England. His English grandmother ruled the family; the English language was at least as familiar to him as the German, and I imagine that he felt, if anything, more at home in an English country house than in a German *Schloss*, even if there was not much to distinguish one from the other. In 1914 he had just finished his studies at Oxford and gone on a trip to Canada when war broke out. Like many of the others he got no farther than Gibraltar in his attempt to reach Germany, and was sent on to Wakefield. It was a particularly cruel situation for him, as it was for all people who had sympathies and interests on both sides and had to try to suppress those conflicting with their duties; and for him not being able to fight made it worse instead of better, for the less he could actually do for his country the less justified did he feel in harbouring any feelings of sympathy for its enemies. He had been extremely happy at Oxford and now felt he had had no right to be; he was torn between conflicting emotions and there could be no satisfactory issue to such a conflict. Thus he had reason to be thoroughly miserable and he was, but in time he developed a quite uncanny gift for making himself very much more miserable even than he need have been. I suppose this was a sort of self-inflicted penance, a piling up of miseries in lieu of those he escaped through taking no part in the fighting, for he would really have loathed the fighting he so ardently wished for in order to do his duty. This may seem very tortuous and involved psychology, but it is a typical example of barbed wire psychology, of barbed wire sickness, from which, as the reader may have discovered, all the men I have described suffered in one way or another, as indeed did all the prisoners. So J. lived in a hut where he likcd no one, in the most desolate part of that desolate North Camp, and spent his time re-reading two books and refusing to take any interest in any others. One was Olive Schreiner's *Story of an African Farm* and the other, *Sinister Street* by Compton Mackenzie. These he declared were unsurpassable masterpieces and others he would be too stupid to understand. I suppose they held some secret message for him, easier to guess at in the second work, but he never explained this. As for his alleged stupidity that was part of his campaign of self-depreciation. Incidentally he was very English in this: he loved to appear a great deal more foolish than he was, and managed so well that most people thought him a quite extraordinarily insignificant though not unpleasant boy. That is a very great gift for a diplomat and J. intended to be one and did become one, too. He looked a very typical product of Oxford at that time, tall, fair and loose-limbed, with tweeds, flannels and accent all complete. Fate was kind to him, for he got into endless trouble, always through no fault of his own, and had as bad a time as he could have wished for. He was involved in an attempt to escape from the camp, which failed, and got into great trouble through a newspaper campaign directed against the wife of a high British official, a great friend of his mother's and a woman of his mother's age, who had come to see him. This was constructed into a love affair (absolutely unthinkable under camp conditions between any visitor and any prisoner, as the papers well knew), and even espionage was hinted at quite openly, so that the husband's position became untenable. A truly abominable affair all round. Needless to say, J. was one of those kept imprisoned many months after the armistice, and only returned home in 1919. He has been a great success as a diplomat in many parts of the world since that time, in the U.S.A, as in Asia, and the last time I saw him was a few months ago in a London cinema where a picture of the Abyssinian coronation was shown. There amongst the other European diplomatic dignitaries he sat, looking as glum as if he was still surveying the melancholy expanse of his camp. For his character has, I think, been stamped by that camp for life; he is happiest away from Europe in the wilds. I think there is every chance that he will achieve very great distinction in his profession, but very little that he will ever enjoy life.

Varied were my friends then, and varied have been their fates. Some have slipped back to their pre-war positions and life, and probably internment has remained to them no more than a very unpleasant episode. Of such is one of my 'taxi-friends' in whose company I spent years, and the only one of the three with whom I became friends really. It was a curious friendship, for we had no common interests and very little to say to each other, but he was most extraordinarily kind to me throughout and I got very fond of him. He was one of those very unassuming and unselfish people who are ever doing something for others and spoil them so that they get very little thanks in return. But he didn't mind that in the least and just went on being serviceable to everybody. He had his reward in being one of the few who remained almost invariably cheerful, and after the war he rejoined his family, took up his job again, and will, I hope, live happily ever after; like another man there who was an ardent Zionist and a happy family-man before the war and is both now; like a third friend of mine, then a young student of medicine and enthusiastic about the new truths of psycho-analysis, now a specialist of growing fame in the U.S.A. Yes, there are such, but there are the others like that son of one of the leading German politicians who committed suicide in 1920 the day before his marriage, and that very wealthy young man from Hamburg who killed himself in South America, for no tangible reasons whatsoever.

And God knows what has become of all the others who were but shadows to me, of all those bored and ordinary businessmen, the quarrelsome strategists who moved flags on maps and killed enemies with their shouting, the nice vacant young men who played tennis, the drunks who went by the general name of the 'Whale-club,' all those types found wherever there is a crowd of men. They remained anonymous to one and one never got to realize them as separate human entities, though one lived in their midst day and night for year after year. No more significant individually than the people one travels with in 'bus or tube and yet an infinitely more important factor in one's life than any individuals could possibly be, for they were that terribly oppressive and inescapable thousandfold monster: the crowd — master of one's destinies while the barbed wire enclosed one, no more than a vague memory once one had left it behind.

Chapter XII
Men Without Women

Even extreme puritans do not deny that there is such a thing as sex, though they may consider it a forbidden or painful subject. The authorities responsible for prisoners' camps apparently gave it no consideration whatsoever. This, I suppose, applies to all prison life, but as so far I have had no experience of peace time and normal prisons I cannot affirm this fact. Apart from prison life, however, in which such treatment may possibly be considered part of the punishment, I can only think of school life or that of monasteries which can be compared to existence in an internment camp in that respect. Soldiers, whether in peace or in war, have their outings, and all armies recognized the need of making some sort of provision for the satisfaction of the sexual needs of the troops. As little as possible was said about this, but puritanical protests were ignored and facts faced. As far as prisoners' camps went, the same facts were not faced, but ignored. No person in their senses could deny that sex plays quite a considerable part in men's lives, from Freudians who think of all life in terms of sex to ascetics who think it a regrettable inconvenience, but the men who invented the prison camp system or those who were responsible for its application treated it simply as nonexistent.

During the years of their imprisonment the interned civilians never came into contact with women except on the infrequent occasions when they received a visit. The visitors sat on one side of a long table, the prisoners on the opposite side, officers between them and armed guards round them. These precautions having been taken, they were allowed a conversation of about twenty-five minutes, after which the visitors had to leave, and when they were safely out of the camp the prisoners were conducted back to their abodes. That was the only form of intercourse between the sexes for the duration of the war in the camps I have known.

I have said that school life and monastic life provide parallels, but this statement needs qualifications. A boy who lives at school does not live there all the year round, he has his holidays in which to meet the female species, besides which he is — rightly or wrongly — supposed to be too young to stand in need of sexual intercourse. The monastery is like the camp in its rigorous exclusion of women and in its disregard of sexual needs, but there is one great difference: monastic chastity is voluntary and self-imposed. Furthermore, both schools and monasteries have evolved disciplinary systems for suppressing or sublimating the sexual urge, they do not simply ignore it. But in spite of these obvious and important differences, sex life in camp had many similarities with that of schoolboys and — I imagine — with that of monks. The furtiveness with which such matters soon began to be treated was schoolboyish and so was the fondness for dirty jokes and talk which was no more than an outlet for unsatisfiable needs, a form of regression. It was rumoured that the tea we got contained some sort of bromide intended to calm passion; whether that was a fact I cannot say, it certainly had an odd sort of taste, nor can I say whether it had any of the desired effect if it was thus composed. In any case, it seems to me a supremely naïve attempt at solving a most arduous problem.

Many hundreds of thousands of men were subjected to similar treatment in all countries, and in most cases they survived it, but how did they survive it and what happened really? I have read several accounts, some very lurid and some very bashful, but they have only convinced me of one thing, that here again one can and must not generalize. One should only speak of things as one experienced them personally, and that again must to a great extent remain guesswork, because even in camp the majority continue to treat their sex life as a private matter. Perhaps even more so than in everyday life where some may be inclined to boast about their love adventures, whereas it is quite certain that in camp there could be nothing to boast about whatever happened.

The first and obvious conclusion anyone considering the matter dispassionately would arrive at is this: when you lock up thousands of men between eighteen and fifty years for a very prolonged period and prevent any intercourse with the opposite sex, you inevitably drive them, indeed, almost force them into homosexual intercourse. As this conclusion would have been considered painful and not good for the ears of the public, the matter was never discussed or even alluded to in the papers, and the whole problem was ignored, but it can and should not be ignored by any writer on the subject of prison life.

The conclusion is, as I said, obvious, but I am not at all sure that it is true. In the sense commonly given to the term homosexuality, that is to say, sexual acts between two of the same sex, it was certainly not true in the camps I have known. Such acts were, I should say, extremely infrequent, and personally I know of none at all. This may seem improbable, and would be more than improbable if there was not one most important point to be considered: the camp offered no possibility of isolation. With the insignificant exception of the few single huts (hardly a dozen) there was no possible privacy for anybody, and such intercourse would have had to be conducted within hearing (if not seeing) of others, and therefore to the general knowledge. Now one of the things camp life has taught me is the quite surprisingly strong sense of shame and reticence between men, which in ordinary life has no occasion to show itself. Whenever they could avoid it, they would not even dress or undress in front of each other; in that respect, as in all others, men clutch at the slightest chance of privacy, and as to their committing sexual acts of any kind while under observation — as they always were — that was almost unthinkable. I read with interest some time ago that elephants share this prejudice and invariably retire to secluded spots on such occasions, so as there are undoubtedly humans who do not find seclusion a *conditio sine qua non*, I will say that the prisoners I knew were elephantine in their habits. I must, however, insist on this being but my personal impression and conviction, while several of my fellow prisoners held quite different views. I have been told, for instance, that in the last year or so homosexuality became almost general at Knockaloe, that some men were put in gaol for it (which would be the real acme of hypocrisy), but though that is quite possible, I cannot say whether it is true or not. To my own knowledge there was nothing of what is called homosexuality, but what I learnt was that homosexuality is not what it is called. It is a complicated and profound phenomenon, and its roots go deeper than sexuality, it is also very difficult to discuss for lack of a precise terminology. The majority limit sexuality to its narrowest sense, and are immensely shocked when it is pointed out to them that there is no hard and sharp division between what they admit to be sexual acts or sensations and a great many other things which they like to consider perfectly 'harmless' or maybe of a spiritual nature. To them homosexuality means an unnatural sin or else a disease, for they believe sexuality to be a sort of definitely circumscribed province of the human personality to which it must remain confined, and any transgression of the boundaries is to them immoral if not criminal, or at the least abnormal, that is to say, diseased. Against them there are arrayed a growing mass of people influenced by the psycho-analysts who teach that sex is everything, and that everything can be reduced, analysed back to a sexual desire. If with the first, sexuality is so narrowly circumscribed that it must limit itself to a few definite acts or else be looked on as criminal and diseased, with the others sexuality becomes so universal a conception that there is no imaginable art, sensation, or relationship, which is not based on sex. Neither opinion is at all helpful, for to the first homosexuality is just an abomination not to be mentioned, or at the least a very painful subject which they wish to ignore, while to the latter it is just a matter of course. The great stumbling block is really the term sex or sexuality. If you call it affection, for example, you will find everyone of the first group quite ready to agree that affection between people of the same sex is the most natural and obvious thing in the world, but that it has nothing in common with sexuality. The truth lies, I think, somewhere between the two extremes. Nothing is entirely unrelated to the sexual, but there are so many varying degrees that there should be a series of differentiating terms. If you go back far enough, which psycho-analysis does, you are bound to arrive at the most primitive bases of human psychological life, and thus you arrive at the sex impulse. You can therefore state as a truth that all human spiritual achievement is an expression of sex and that all human relationships are of sexual nature; this is not untrue, but it is only part of the truth. Things of common origin are not therefore similar; without manure you cannot grow roses, but a rose is not the same as manure, or even as its leaf or the stem of its tree or its roots. Everything is derived from the sex impulse, is of sexual nature in its origin, but may be so far removed from that origin that there is no longer any similarity.

The point of view of those who would narrowly circumscribe sex life may be dismissed as false and as conventional, for such conventions vary from age to age and clime to clime, but the point of view of their antagonists cannot be accepted either: it is too superficial. It is not only based on what is but a half-truth, but it simply does not go deep enough into the matter. It considers all as derived from sexual impulse, which is true, but it considers sexual impulse itself as primitive and underived, which it is not. If you accept the beliefs of science as psycho-analysts profess to do, you cannot stop at human psychology in your attempt at explanation. Nothing divides what used to be called inanimate matter from animate, the mineral from the vegetable kingdom, or that from the animal, and sex as we understand it only makes an appearance rather high up in the scale. The most primitive and universal impulses we know are those of attraction and repulsion, the most primitive and universal tendencies of forces we consider the positive and negative, which act on each other, and from them all seems derived. In all life there is the will to live and to grow, all is attracted to what furthers growth, repulsed by what hinders it, is therefore inclusive and exclusive. Love and hate are the names given to these impulses when we come to human relationships; humans love (instinctively) what furthers growth, hate what hinders it. But there are innumerable degrees between the mutual attraction and repulsion of, let us say, electrons, and human love and hate. Hunger, for instance, the animal desire for suitable nourishment, is somewhere between the two, and it is a much more primitive impulse than the sexual. There are in sex life plenty of traces of its derivation from that more primitive impulse, and yet more traces in language. In its desire for expansion each human being is instinctively attracted by all that furthers it, repelled by what hinders it, that and not sex is the real basis of man's relations with all the world outside himself. Every being is and feels incomplete and seeks for what can complete it, and that is of infinitely manifold nature. In the higher (or what we call the higher) forms of life there is a division into two sexes, attractive and complementary to each other, and with that sexuality as we know it enters life. But it is not the simple thing it seems, for it goes back far deeper and is not divorced from any other urge of growth. No male is simply male, no female simply female; one is not purely positive and the other negative, one not active and the other not passive entirely. Every human is of mixed composition and what he needs to complete him is equally mixed. If at one end you have the pure and exclusively male and at the other the pure and exclusively female they would form a perfect whole, but they do not exist. Instead of that you have all sorts of mixtures of the elements, in which as a rule one predominates: in most men the masculine element is much stronger than the feminine; in most women the feminine much stronger than the masculine, but there are both in all. A predominantly masculine nature will seek one where the feminine predominates, but such a predominantly masculine nature may belong to a person of the female sex and a predominantly feminine one to a person of the male sex. I think, therefore, that one of the profounder truths of homosexuality is that it is based on the universal and normal need for that which completes the individual and which it does not invariably find in the opposite sex. But in the vast majority of such cases the people concerned would consider that the sexual element does not enter at all into their relationships.

For many reasons, of convention, education, and heredity, such homosexuality would not lead to anything approaching sexual intercourse and would go by the name of friendship, comradeship, mutual sympathy. It need not be sexual at all in the ordinary sense of the word, but in my opinion that is really a side issue. What I have been trying to show is that the sexual appetite is but one form or derivation of a deeper and more essentially vital instinct, that of growth, of self-fulfilment by the complementary.

That instinct is ever present and at work, but most strongly in youth — a youth which lasts as long as the desire for growth, that is to say, all their life with some people and but a short time with others, but while it lasts the search continues. Outer circumstances cannot change its nature, but they may alter its direction, and such outer circumstances are those of a prisoners' camp.

I must apologize for having strayed far from my theme, but this digression is necessary to its comprehension. All such problems are and will probably ever remain controversial, and I do not offer my explanations as the only possible ones. They are besides necessarily incomplete and sketchy, for it would need a volume to exhaust the subject, but my object is not to write a treatise on the problem of homosexuality, but to explain the nature of relationships between a crowd of men deprived of all non-masculine companionship for years. I give my interpretation of what I have seen, one which I believe to be true.

The basic fact is that a human being is self-sufficient in only a very few exceptional cases. All the vast majority need other human beings, need human intercourse and human affection. Plato's myth of the hermaphrodite split in halves and ever seeking the wanting half is a very profound one, every human is incomplete and seeks completion through another. That other as a rule belongs to the opposite sex, thus a rather masculine woman will prefer a rather feminine man, but possibly another woman. What does this really amount to, what is it we call masculine or feminine characters? Active and passive seem to me more just terms, because divorced from sex proper. Attraction is a polar force. There are characters whose instinct is to conquer, to vanquish, to dominate, but also to protect, to care and provide for, active natures, and active, therefore, as well in their sexuality, 'masculine' natures, and the opposite ones wishing to be protected, directed, and willing to be courted and conquered, 'feminine' characters. But these characters do not necessarily correspond to the physique or the sex; there are very delicate women of very active masculine character and very athletic young males of very passive feminine mentality. The mutual attraction between the active and the passive you will find in every school among boys whose sexuality proper is still dormant; always there are protectors and protected, leaders and led. Age plays an important part in such relationships, the younger liking to submit to the leadership of the elder. And you will find exactly the same kind of relationships in a prisoners' camp where there are men of different ages. There will be a sort of retrogression to that boyish mutual affection, to strongly emotional friendships that rarely find expression in words. There were a great many such friendships of a more or less affectionate nature, furthered by the intimacy of life in common. Often the partner's age differed a good deal, for what is more natural than the intense admiration of a boy of nineteen thrown together with 'wise' and experienced men of thirty or more? But there were many as well where the partners were of equal age but had complementary natures. In most cases, I think that under normal circumstances one of the partners would have belonged to the feminine sex; cases like the classical example of the countess and the page in *Figaro* or the similar figures in *Rosenkavalier*, for instance; here both partners belonged of necessity to the same sex, but that did not seem essential.

I think that the elder married men did not enter into all this, partly because they were elder and their growth had come to a stop, partly because the memory of their wives remained vivid in spite of their absence, nor is it possible to say how many others remained unaffected. But there certainly were a very great number of friendly couples considered to belong together. I could not say how far any of them were self-conscious, for — strange as this may appear — I have never heard this question discussed, but facts were silently accepted.

One thing I learnt in camp life is that nearly all men have an infinitely greater desire for and power of affection and tenderness than they could ever be got to admit to others or even to themselves, just as I learned how easily and strongly they hate. Men are very much more emotional and irrational, and very much less 'grown-up' than they are supposed to be or wish to appear. That side of their character is in everyday life revealed to their family only or else to their intimates, but here in a way everyone was intimate. Man is incapable of being happy without making others happy; he must — according to his nature — protect, care for, 'mother' others or let himself be cared for and guided. But as everyone's nature is mixed, he generally needs both. A very happily married and wise friend of mine once explained to me the basis of that happiness. A man in me is married to a woman in her and a woman in me to a man in her.

That I consider a profound saying; sexuality in the ordinary and limited sense is very much of a surface phenomenon, but the need for human love is deep. Most people's lives are in reality filled by the love and life of one other human or more than one. Man cannot and should not (as the Bible says) live alone; that is, incidentally, why single confinement is of inhuman cruelty. No prison, no compulsion can change man's nature in that respect. Where for outer reasons or inner (constitutional) reasons the normal solution is impossible, that is to say, where the need for love and that for sexual fulfilment cannot be achieved together as between man and woman, that need will find other ways of expression, that love will flow into different channels. Psycho-analysis has coined the term sublimation for the transformation of what might have remained sexual into another and higher form of activity. The power of emotion is directed into impersonal and more universal love, that is why there are 'saints' amongst nurses and teachers and all sorts of humanitarians; that is also why humans who find neither other humans or causes to love spend their emotion on cats and dogs. All that *is* not simply sexuality, but all that may grow from what sexuality has not absorbed. And after all, all religious precepts of chastity, in particular the celibacy of the Catholic priesthood, monastic life of the Christians or Yogha of the Hindus are founded on this recognition of the possibility of sublimation of sexuality.

The direction of the sexual instinct into other channels than the normal was enforced in prisoners' camps. The most obvious change would have been a simple change of object, a transference of sexual love to the own sex. I began by saying that in spite of its obviousness this was very rare in my opinion. Amongst the elder men a good many did not worry much about sexuality, amongst the younger the coarser took refuge in dirty jokes, possibly in certain acts. Amongst the majority the instinct took the form of friendships. These did not, I think, lead to acts of a sexual nature, but I have been at pains to explain that I think this an irrelevant aspect of the problem. Amongst a minority there was sublimation of a more intellectual nature, devotion to work, to research, to spiritual experiments of a more than ordinarily emotional nature, bordering in some cases on insanity. But if there was sublimation, there was also its opposite leading to brutalization and bestiality.

Whichever way you look at it, you cannot deny that relationships among prisoners as among all men are predominantly of an emotional nature. Barbed wire was responsible for an all-pervading atmosphere of hate; it was also responsible for the birth of a great deal of love, and the manifestations of both hate and love were conditioned by it, were of a peculiar nature, were as far removed from the normal, conventional, and usual as was all that existence. It would be interesting to know how far the influence of those years in a prison camp has been a permanent one, but there is no answer to that question. On the whole I am inclined to think that most of the young men, below perhaps twenty-three, have been permanently influenced or definitely modelled by it, while to the older men who were more settled it has remained more of an episode. But all of them have learnt, or should have learnt, this lesson: sexuality in the narrow sense goes much less deep than one is inclined to think and flows into other channels when forced to by circumstances, but the need for love never dies. Attraction and repulsion are at the basis of life. It oscillates between love and hatred, and in a prison camp between the hatred bred by enforced community and the love which counteracts that hatred.

Chapter XIII
Painting

There were few lucky enough to be able to continue working at their usual profession after they had been interned. The majority were without any occupation at all or had to try to find some work which would keep them occupied. That could be found, but what was more difficult to achieve was the conviction that this new-found work had any sense at all, because, as a matter of fact, it really had none in most cases. If a middle-aged businessman did assiduously follow lectures on the policy of Bismarck or a young medical student took piano lessons they could not but feel after a time that they had strayed from their road in life and taken paths that led nowhere in particular. They were just wasting their time and could find no satisfaction in their work; it would not increase the one's business or business capabilities, it would not help the other to pass his exams. That is why I considered myself very fortunate in being an artist, for if there was a very great deal of work I could not go on with in camp, yet there remained a number of possibilities. I had to adapt myself to circumstances, but I need not and did not feel that I was utterly wasting my time. I could continue to work and therefore to make progress in an art, which was — as I then believed — my chief interest in life.

I have already described how I managed to force myself to work under very trying circumstances in Knockaloe. After that all should have been plain sailing, but as a matter of fact it was not. For a long time I found it impossible to do any work in Wakefield; I had to get used to the idea of being definitely a prisoner, of knowing no other life or surroundings for a period that stretched away into a dim, incalculable distance. All energy and willpower seemed to have left me there; I hated my condition and my camp, I gave myself up to despair, I had not even the wish to start work again. Moreover, mine was not work of a mechanical nature; even if I had wanted to I could not just have sat down and started on it. My favourite work was entirely imaginative in inspiration. Something set me off — it might be a tune, the line of a poem, the movement of a body, or no more than some bits of colour, and it had to be given expression. The actual subject of such-and-such a coloured drawing or miniature was unimportant to me; often I could not have defined it all. What I felt had to take on some sort of shape, human, architectural, or ornamental, and then began the second part of the work, the technical, sketches for the design and composition, essays of colour-schemes, and finally the very slow and laborious execution. It was curious work, and in its meaning often quite as incomprehensible to myself as to others. I had exhibited samples of it sometimes and it had found very few admirers, but these very enthusiastic, while the majority thought the dubious result did not justify the very great labour it had necessitated. Looking back on it now it seems to me the work of a stranger I barely remember having known, and of curiously mixed character. As far as its technique goes, it has little originality, it is derived from Persian, to a lesser degree from Far Eastern art, and it has, in fact, sometimes been taken for such. But as far as the emotions expressed by means of that technique go, they are of a purely personal nature, confused dreams, or sometimes nightmares, often so vague that painting is too intellectual a form of expression for them and music would have served better, often circumscribed in purely decorative pattern-work. They are a manifestation of a troubled and uneasy state of mind that seeks an outlet, and when I look at them now they no longer seem to me, as they did at the time, purely personal, but very characteristic and typical of the anxious unrest, the sense of unknown menace overhanging the years immediately preceding the war, of that atmosphere overcharged with electricity like that before the break of a thunderstorm, which oppressed and unsettled the more sensitive and impressionable, the 'artists' of all countries, though none of them could have explained the exact nature of their presentiments.

As a rule, pre-war times are contrasted with those of the war and after-war as a period not only of peace and plenty but of settled quietude, but that division is wrong. Unrest began long before 1914; social and moral conventions, scientific and artistic creeds were in full dissolution and the change of the 'old order of things' in full progress, only the masses were not yet aware of it, and only a minority had been affected. All that is considered characteristic of the after-war time, and looked on as consequence of war, was already in being. The war interrupted a process of dissolution, evolution was arrested by it and in many ways it temporarily modified, but the after-war at once took up the pre-war legacy, which had gathered speed. The break-up of the old order begun before the war became clear to all after it. In science, philosophy or art, in music or architecture, all that in 1930 still passes for new, modern, revolutionary was in existence before 1914, no new movement of basic importance has appeared after the war, and the same applies to the more superficial and obvious phenomena: motoring, flying and speed-mania, the cinema and exotic music, the craving for the sensational and for eternal change. All these new movements and new inventions and new sensations signified and brought about the end of an epoch of civilization, or, if one prefers to look to the future, the beginning of a new order. But between one order and the next there is a reign of disorder, that reign began sometime in the years before the war, it affected me, as was but natural, and my works of art were but the expression of an inner and personal state of disorder and unrest corresponding to the general.

The war was like a stunning blow which brought every movement not directly connected with it to a standstill, but movements contain accumulated speed which makes them continue for some time after the original impulse is spent, and in that way I, too, had continued my artistic expression. The shock of realization of my condition experienced at Wakefield brought this to a stop, but not to a definite stop yet, for after some months I began anew.

A Paris publisher had decided to bring out a dozen drawings of mine as an accompaniment to Baudelaire's *Fleurs du Mal* — for they were not illustrations. I had left those already finished with him in Paris (where they and he got lost) and decided to do the three or four still needed for the cycle (which were to get lost later), because it gave me a feeling of 'business as usual.' As there were no signs of a return to normality when they were finished I started a series of six biblical subjects, but not of a very saintly character. There was, of course, a Salomé, for she was a sort of presiding goddess of the period, after the works of Gustave Moreau, Oscar Wilde, and Richard Strauss; there was a Judith, and one inspired by the Song of Solomon; there were also a David and Jonathan, an Annunciation, and the sixth never got done; and they were all very rich, very *précieux* and very oriental. They certainly served as an escape from reality (to which the psycho-analysts would limit the function of all art), for during the good many hours a day they kept me busy, only noises, bumps, and vibrations recalling my surroundings to me.

After these there was a long pause, and then came a number of works connected more directly with what was occupying my thoughts at that time, and of which I shall have more to say later; but I was not idle during that pause. It was long, I believe, but I am not sure, for by that time I had lost count of weeks and of months, nor could I then see and comprehend the inner logic of my work, and it seemed to me quite fortuitous whether I did any work or what sort of work I did. Oil painting was difficult on account of its cumbersome implements, so I began to try watercolour work and found that difficult medium very fascinating for landscape painting. At first it seemed to me that there was really very little to paint; the camp itself, though I did try one or two of its aspects, was really very hopeless, and it got more and more hopeless from a painter's point of view as its original aspect of a waste piece of land changed into one of suburban primness; but then spring came along and I discovered that spring in an internment camp had great beauties. There is a saying 'one cannot see the wood for trees,' but the camp had so very few 'trees' that one discovered the 'wood.' I have never watched and lived the coming of spring so intensely as during the months following my first winter, which had meant a very hard time, at Wakefield. Everything took on a quite extraordinary value; there were a few fruit trees in flower outside the wire in the commandant's garden, there was one little laburnum tree, a shabby little thing really, but it seemed a miracle. Then the chestnuts flanking the camp were full of little flowering pyramids, some nasturtiums appeared actually within the wires, and occasionally visitors brought flowers to one man or another. And every tree, every single flower, almost every blade of grass seemed a discovery and something infinitely precious that first spring. So there was lots to paint, and it was work of a kind I had never done before. I remember one incident which at the time impressed me strongly. I was finishing a sketch of the chestnuts running alongside the camp and a man was looking at my work over my shoulder (needless to say, someone always was). And after a while he said: 'You have forgotten the barbed wire,' meaning that I had omitted the ugly lines of wire cutting across the trees. So I had, and what is more, I had not even noticed them! 'Yes,' I said, 'I have forgotten the barbed wire,' and the accent was on the 'forgotten.'

Spring and summer passed, they always seemed to pass in a few days; it was winter again, but I had found another type of work to keep me busy. There was a drawing class by that time, and some man or other sat as a model. I began to do pencil portraits and then a series of caricatures. Of these I had done a great number in former years in Paris, and there was plenty of material for that sort of work where I was now, though by no means all people were willing to be caricatured or liked the results. All this work of varying character was done during what I have called a pause in my imaginative work; and when I come to think of it, I believe that pause must have lasted well over a year, for I remember adding a new variety in the second year, before I returned to my original methods. Quite a number of men were doing inlay work in different woods, and though the work was mostly an eyesore, the woods employed were very pretty. I often watched one of these men at work, and one day I discovered what to do with the thin plaques of wood left over and thrown away, and began collecting them.

No less a person than Leonardo da Vinci has advised painters to gaze at walls or stones, for faces and scenes will arise out of them if you know how to look. The same applies to bits of inlay wood as I had discovered, though not, of course, to all of them. You put them up in front of you and after a time the lines of the grain will reveal their sense. They suggest the picture, and the real art is to add as little as possible, just enough to emphasize the hidden design, an art akin to the painting of China and Japan, where the ground, the silk or paper, is never covered by paint all over, but left to play a most important part in the work of art itself. Thus some small wooden plaque became a seashore or rocks beneath water, the desert with the suggestion of a few low, square houses on the horizon; some were covered with strange plants, cuttings out of a primeval forest, and the biggest and most marvellous of all held the Tibetan Desert and fantastic ruined walls of a city on a hill. But if in spite of intense and prolonged gazing the wood would reveal no secret, I ceased to be Far Eastern and acting as a European barbarian just painted something on it which took no notice at all of its character. The last of these efforts was executed in winter and it was a winter scene. The lines were those of ploughed fields, covered lightly with snow by a little white watercolour paint; the sky was left almost the colour of the wood, and there was a bare black tree near the horizon which was a cheating addition. It is a melancholy little thing, a real barbed wire product. After this the charm no longer operated, and all pieces of wood again looked alike to me.

Thus did one exhaust one possibility after another, and when one had come to the end, deep depression followed and lasted until the next phase. Things did not repeat themselves: the flowers of the second spring only said: 'How many more springs?' There was no new angle from which to look at the scenery. All faces worth recording had been drawn, all caricatures accomplished. All wood was just wood. It was then that with a kind of desperation I once more took up my imaginative work, but I found its character had altered. It had taken on a new meaning and one I myself could not fathom at the time. It had, in fact, ceased to have any artistic signification, it had taken on a mystic character about which I shall have more to say in a later chapter.

Chapter XIV
The Stage

I had been very much mixed up with the theatre in the period immediately preceding my internment and so I was naturally very interested in theatricals and their development in the camp. When I first came to Wakefield both the South Camp and the North already possessed 'companies,' but things were very badly done and most amateurish. They were, however, destined to develop to a most extraordinary degree, and some of the shows I saw there towards the end of my stay were as good as any you could see outside the wire. Conditions were, of course, very different. In a normal theatrical venture the first thing to settle is the play, and having decided on a play you engage the actors fit for the parts, whereas in camp you had to take the talent available for a basis and then try to find a play with parts for which you could find protagonists. You could not find actors to suit the parts, you had to find parts to suit the actors, for very few of them were versatile enough to go beyond what was naturally akin to them. But within these limits they were or rather became, extremely able, and what they lacked in technique and experience they made up for by enthusiasm. Even in normal life actors are far more ambitious and harder workers than members of any other profession — speaking generally. As a rule they really have very little life outside their art; when they are not acting they are looking at acting (and bemoaning the fact that they are not on the stage themselves), and that incidentally is why actors are as a rule extremely dull people to know for anyone who is not himself a stage enthusiast. There is something very childlike about the typical actor's mentality: it is all a game of make-believe and dress-up, and I think that anyone sufficiently 'grown-up' or serious to look at the stage rationally could never make a good actor, director, or producer. In camp that natural indifference of the actor to all outside the theatre was intensified for the simple reason that everyone there tried hard, in self-defence, to persuade himself of the real importance of the work he had undertaken in order to forget its inherent futility, and so the actors found no work too much for them. The more rehearsals, the better they liked it, and they were extremely ambitious, and if you take their natural limitations into consideration you will understand how a group of specialists developed, each of whom was really excellent in his particular and strictly limited manner.

Certainly the most astonishing among the actors were those that specialized in female parts, and they never ceased to surprise me. At first, what you saw on the stage were men rather clumsily disguised as women and about as convincing as the disguised undergraduates of *Charley's Aunt*, but this changed very quickly and they developed into very plausible actresses. This was all the more remarkable as hardly any of them were of a type at all feminine originally. We had one Viennese boy who physically, at least, was not inappropriate, having very small hands, feet, wrists, and rather a high voice, though there was nothing feminine in his character, and his speciality was what would now be called 'vamp' parts, only the term had not yet been invented. The only other man at all feminine in appearance I remember specialized in parts of old women and was extremely good in them, but our greatest actress, really remarkable in tragic parts, was originally very much of an athlete. He came from one of the Hanseatic towns, looked bursting with health, and was very good at and enthusiastic about all games. I don't know how he ever came to be cast for a female part, but he was a success from the start and later on really powerful. He was tremendously hardworking, and his evolution was really curious and one of the most convincing proofs I have seen of the predominance of the intellectual or spiritual over the physical. '*Es ist der Geist, der sich den Körper baut*' (It is the spirit which builds itself its body) is a famous saying of Schiller's, the truth of which impressed me then; for as that youth became more and more of what I do not hesitate to call a great actress on the stage, he also became more and more feminine off the stage, and after some years of this he no longer played hockey or football or whatever it used to be but walked about mincingly with a little dog, called Toutou, with a pink bow. I used to think that he and some of the others would end by developing truly feminine physical characteristics if the war lasted long enough. This was a case of quite exceptional futility of effort. For what could all this mean for them in later life? But the thought never seemed to strike them, and even in their rivalry they became as catty and intriguing as if they had been real primadonnas. I have often wondered how they fared when they returned to normal life, to their offices or studies. Meanwhile, they were admirable on the stage, or at least seemed so, for another thing to be considered is the adaptation of the public to extraordinary conditions. There were no real women to compare them to; one saw none, or so seldom that the impression did not last. When I look at some of the snapshots I possess, the 'leading ladies' look rather absurd to me now, but they did not look so at the time, and I also remember that when a woman friend of mine visited me at Wakefield her voice seemed very curious to me and it was very difficult to hear what she said, for the voice seemed so unnaturally high! That is why I hesitate to say whether the acting in camp was really as good as it seemed to me — there was no possibility of comparison; but I do know that when I saw some of the plays I had seen at Wakefield done on the regular German stage and by well-known actors, these seemed poor in comparison with the camp artists. That was my impression of *Alt-Heidelberg* (known in England as *The Student Prince*), where one of our ex-officers was truly remarkable in the title-part, of *Taifun*, where our 'vamp' distinguished herself, and of some Sudermann plays where I remember our great *tragédienne* and our most distinguished *père-noble* or 'heavy father.'

It was really rather admirable in its way, especially considering the fact that there could never be more than two representations of a play, and more often there was but one, after which all the work and all the anxiety would begin again; for one never knew what might not happen before the next show. Anyone might commit some sort of crime and the show would be prohibited, or the people of the neighbouring camps not allowed to attend and the show become a financial failure. I think that the actors, and next to them the musicians, were the happiest people in camp, and certainly they contributed more to the happiness of the rest than anyone else. If anybody doubts whether art is of real importance in life, which the majority of 'common-sense' people are very much inclined to do, a course of prison life might very quickly induce them to modify their opinions.

It was while the stage was as yet in a very primitive condition that I decided on my first theatrical venture, for the memory of my work at the opera was still fresh, and I was tempted to try to see what could be done in that line, costume and scenery, under camp conditions. After due deliberation I decided on a cabaret show, for that would give scope for a certain display of costumes, and it would allow me to utilize such talent as I thought I could find amongst the people I knew or knew of. This was my first contact with the administration and what one might call the public life of the place and it taught me a lot about it. I cannot say that it was a pleasant experience, but it was certainly instructive. The people I had approached with a view to their appearance in my programme were very pleased and eager, for it gave them something to do and to think about; but I had imagined in my innocence of heart and ignorance of camp psychology that everybody would be delighted with the idea and that was quite a mistaken notion. Here was I ready to do all the work and take the responsibility of success or failure without asking anything in return; the receipts were to cover the cost of the enterprise, and if there was any money left over it was to go to the stage fund. I was going to give the people entertainment of a new sort and which would be, I knew, better done and far less amateurish, within the limits imposed by conditions, than anything that had yet been attempted. It seemed to me everyone ought to be delighted and eager to help. But everyone was not. As the West Camp possessed no stage I wanted that of the North Camp, which incidentally provided most of the artists that were to appear, and here I met with the first resistance. They could not refuse the stage for the performance because that had been permitted by the commandant, but I could never get it for the necessary rehearsals. It just could never be put at my disposal when I could gather together the artists (which necessitated a series of 'permits' and 'passes' each time). After a time I began to understand that I had come up against professional jealousy! They thought this an attempt to found a new and rival stage and that by a 'foreigner' from the West Camp. Well, I had rehearsals where and when I could. Then some of the leading lights of the committee of members of the different camps I had formed resigned under various pretexts. I was told that the show was considered too luxurious, that it would call forth adverse criticism, that the commandant was against its taking place. This I ascertained to be quite untrue. Then I was warned that there was great hostility because the costumes had all been ordered from Poiret in Paris! This rather staggered me, considering M. Poiret's prices and the twenty or thirty pounds we could raise for the show, but it also put my back up, for I had at last grasped that there was a deliberate campaign of calumny and ill will on foot. When they found that did not work they came out with their last and strongest argument: everybody, they said, except, of course, they themselves who knew me personally, was convinced that I was getting up that show solely to put money in my pockets, they were preparing a hostile demonstration and the only thing for me to do was to countermand the show and drop it altogether. That was actually on the day before the performance was to take place. To this I replied that I could not prevent hostile demonstrations, but that nothing would induce me to desist from holding my show except an order which would force me to, and that it did not worry me at all if I was suspected of putting money in my pocket, as my accounts were to be made public. All the bills had to pass through the camp bank, all the receipts were taken by the theatre officials of the North Camp, and I would insist that the results of both sums spent and received as certified by the controlling agencies, should be made public immediately after the show and posted up in each camp. There was a curious silence after my declaration, and at that moment it suddenly dawned on me that their last interference had not been pure bluff but that they had really believed I was getting up the show for my own benefit and were dumbfounded at the discovery of my simple-mindedness. In fact, they had thought the whole thing a *Schiebung* if a somewhat elaborate one, for could there be anything in 'public' life that was not a *Schiebung*?[1]

---

1 I have related these experiences somewhat at length, not because they were of great importance, but because they furnish a most characteristic example of the curious twists and turns of barbed wire psychology.

Now at last my eyes were open, and I felt very sick and disgusted. But I was determined to go through with this, and the curtain rose punctually the next evening before a crowded hall and with the commandant and some officers in the first row. After the first scene, when the curtain fell, the applause was deafening, and by the time the end came the hall fairly shook. The show had to be repeated on three evenings and could have gone on longer if one could have got permission for that. It was, in fact, a triumph, the first stage triumph the camp had known. I was immensely relieved, of course, but I had had enough of public life. Certainly, no one was more charming and complimentary than my ex-enemies; of course, I was urged to continue my activities (which had brought quite a nice little sum to the fund), but I only smiled politely and refused. I was sorry to in a way, because I loved the work, but I felt thoroughly disgusted with humanity and a nervous wreck into the bargain.

I do not remember all the different scenes or numbers I produced, and the designs for the costumes are lost like nearly everything referring to that period, but a good deal of the show has remained in my memory. I adhered throughout the show to the principle of extremely simple and neutral scenery to set off costumes as colourful and apparently rich as possible. The stage was transformed into a semicircle formed by curtains which were grey in some scenes and black in others, and made of extremely cheap cotton which had an attractive sheen. There were two very large garden vases on pedestals made of white plaster and filled with stiff paper roses on either side of the stage, and where a scene demanded any furniture that consisted of couches, covered with the stuff the curtains were made of, and a few small round tabourets of wood and cardboard painted white. The costumes were, of course, no more than a compromise. I had sent my designs to the firm which had made my costumes for the opera, but in this case it would have been far too expensive to have costumes made to order, so they were simply hired, and they sent me the nearest approaches they had in stock to what I wanted to have. Some were really quite good, some others very far indeed removed from my dreams, but for the eyes of Wakefield it was a vision of unheard-of, almost dreamlike beauty, and even to my own more critical eyes the pictures really looked rather lovely after having been starved of colour, light, and brilliance for so very long.

The first scene was a Mozart scene. Three musicians in the costumes of the period, several ladies and gentlemen were assembled on the stage when the curtain rose. A Mozart Trio was played, and very well played by our professional virtuosos, a minuet (the Don Giovanni music) was danced by two couples, and after that a tenor appeared and sang two or three Mozart songs rather charmingly, and the curtain fell slowly with the last notes. This was the longest and most complete scene, and I had placed it first because I believed that it must decide the success of the evening, as it eventually did. Its standard was really high, for I knew that as far as music went we really had something to show one need not be ashamed of, and also that I should get good costumes of that period. They were very charming, the wigs too and the makeup were good. The weakest part of that scene was certainly the dancing, for there was not much eighteenth-century grace or *talon rouge* to be found in camp, but even that was not as bad as it might have been, and it certainly got a good deal of applause.

It was very much better in some of the other scenes. I remember a Viennese waltz with costumes and music of the time of the Vienna Congress, one of the dancers being Viennese, which was a great performance. The colour scheme was sky-blue, white, and gold, the man wearing a uniform of the period, and it had to be repeated twice. There were modern dances, modern at the time: a tango, a foxtrot, a Boston, and a one-step by two couples in black and white before a black background, and there were two mute scenes, between a mimodrama[2] and a dance scene, one being Persian and the other of the Pierrot and Columbine variety. There was also a 'funny man,' whom I needed when a change of scenery was necessary and whom I thought anything but funny. His humour appealed to the audience though and so did another man who read or recited poetry.

I was very glad when it was all over, but I felt very 'out-of-work' for some time, though not sufficiently so to embark on other ventures of the kind. I refused a number of propositions, and then people forgot about me and the two stages proceeded on their way. The North became the more serious and far the better of the two, but the South also had some very good productions, for which they borrowed the 'stars' from their rival; their special line, however, remained farce of a somewhat heavy kind. Only our unfortunate West never got any further because we had no stage and the others would not lend theirs. That was no doubt why the West objected to my resting on my laurels and why I decided on a new venture after more than two years' resistance and a good deal of thinking the matter over.

This, I decided, should be carried out in the West Camp, for I would never again make myself dependent on outside goodwill, so I could only dispose of a small platform and could have no scenery. Nor did I intend to make my fate dependent on what all manner of people unknown to me thought right or wrong, so in the end I formed a club. All we had to ask of the camp was to let us use the tent one night a month and that was easy as it was hardly ever used at night. Even that favour created a certain amount of animosity, but as I now took that for granted, I did not care much, especially as anyone in our camp was free to become a member, while only men I knew and asked to join would come from the other camps. They had to pay a monthly contribution

---

2 A drama performed in mime.

to cover the costs, and any money left over would go on to the next month's accounts to be rendered to the club. As the tent was not large, there could be only a very limited number of members, about eighty if I remember right. My plans were modest enough in externals: a small hall, a most primitive stage, a small audience, and small cost, but they were all the more ambitious artistically, for this was to be a small stage of the kind which the Germans label *Kammerspiele* and the French *studio*. I would have one-act or very short plays, chamber music of the best, possibly dancing. I had quite a list of plays I wanted to act, but as I could only get them in English, I had first of all to translate them. They included plays by Tagore, Strindberg, Chekov, Andreief, Shaw, and Japanese Nô plays. The whole thing was to be a friendly sort of affair with the members (who included all my personal friends) to have their say in the matter.

I had the number of members required and their subscriptions in a very few days, for I had some very energetic and enthusiastic supporters, the programme was settled and the rehearsals began. The first programme of the new enterprise had two numbers, chamber music first, a trio, a 'cello solo, a piano solo, all modern music, and after that a one-act play by Evreinof called *The Happy Death* which I considered and still consider a little masterpiece. It is a modern and highly ironical Harlequinade with a good deal of depth to it, the characters of which are the classical Pierrot, Harlequin, and Columbine with the addition of a Doctor and of Death, dressed as a veiled figure in hooped skirts. My curtains still existed; I had grey curtains, a couch, a plain table and two plain chairs and a piece of cardboard painted to represent a clock on the stage. All the figures had the traditional cheap costumes and Death wore what had once been one of my black curtains. The little serio-comic play was very charmingly acted, and when it had ended with the Dance of Death executed by the veiled figure and Pierrot to the tune of a majestic old Pavane, played by the 'cello behind the curtains, the enthusiasm was so great that I was dragged on to the platform and had to make a short speech. It is the only speech I have ever made, nor do I ever wish to make another. The audience was satisfied with it, though, and so this evening ended very harmoniously, and it was only later that I heard that some people had grumbled because I held a cigarette in my fingers when addressing them, which they considered a mark of disrespect to the audience.

After the success of the first show I could have had thrice as many members if there had been room or if one had decided on a repetition of the shows, but I did not want them, for nearly all the people who cared for what I wanted to produce belonged to the club, and they made the best audience one could hope to find there. So we started on the second programme. The second evening was to be one of surprises, and called itself 'An Evening in a Cafe.' The hut had tables and chairs as in a café and coffee was served; there was a band on the stage which played Strauss and Offenbach, and the centre of the hall was left empty. I had found a play, the scene of which is laid in a café and another one by Strindberg which could be made to take place in a café. So the actors suddenly appeared out of nowhere and played in the centre of the room. There was but one difficulty, that there could be no prompter. I can remember nothing whatsoever about the first play, except that it was a cheerful sort of affair and that people laughed a lot; the second one was *The Other Woman*, a Strindberg play which is, in effect, a dialogue between two women, reduced to a monologue by the fact that one remains mute. It is a brilliant *tour de force* and it was very well rendered by our local 'vamp.' Altogether it was a very amusing and successful evening.

The third show was to be the most ambitious attempted yet. There was to be a Tagore play called *The Toghi* and a Japanese Nô-play. I had translated them both, and their production would be interesting. For the Tagore play I was to have the help of a man who had lived in India for many years and been a professor at one of the universities there; for the second I should have to rely on my own notions and on the little I had seen of Japanese acting. It would certainly not be a correct rendering, but it should be a curious and fascinating performance. We were all very deeply engrossed in that work, and I was looking forward to the first night much as I had looked forward to the first night of *Carmen* nearly three years earlier, for we were then in February 1918. But once again fate intervened. The first time it had suddenly kicked me into a prisoners' camp; the second time it just as suddenly kicked me out of it. That third show of the theatre club never took place, and the club itself became no more than a dim memory.

Chapter XV
Minor Events and Major

It has been said that it is not events that happen to us but that we come across events, and certainly the latter is a better rendering of the impression produced on us. We pursue a road, it seems to us, and encounter people or events on our progress; rightly or wrongly our impression is that we are moving. That is why in our memory one event, one experience takes its definite place before or after others. You remember that two years ago you went to Paris, that it was before then you published your book and after the journey that you got engaged, etc. But as soon as there is no change, all that alters, for without change time ceases to count, and that is why the years of my captivity have not remained in my memory as a succession of happenings, but rather as something static. It was really a static condition to a very great extent, and if the other years of my life seem like the flowing on of a river those years seem like a stagnant pool. Of course, its waters were ruffled quite frequently, but, looking back, these interruptions seem much more simultaneous than successive in time, all of which is but another way of saying that there was no time. There was movement, as there was life, but movement which seemed without direction, like that of a boat swaying about, moved by winds and waves, but all the time at anchor. There were events, both outer happenings and inner experiences, but I find it difficult to remember their sequence. Did this happen before that? — was it the summer of the second year? — or the autumn of the third? — I could not say any more than a man can say, on waking, which of his half-remembered dreams he dreamed first. Time, in fact, is just as unreal in the monotony of camp life as it is in a dream, and the events and happenings stand out as vaguely as the sensations of moments when one is half awake between one dream and another.

They were such very insignificant happenings, such minute events when considered from outside and from far away, but that again is relative and a mere question of proportion. In a quiet life a letter or a visitor or even a stranger passing by the window assumes great importance and is discussed for weeks; in an agitated life dozens or hundreds of such incidents occur in a few hours, produce no impression at all, and are not considered worth mentioning. There, existence was lethargic, so every slight ripple produced an effect of considerable disturbance, of a brief awakening followed by renewed lethargy. It was a disturbing event to write one's weekly letter, even to make out one's weekly washing-list; it was an event sufficient to mark a day when you received a letter or a parcel and were half-incredulously reminded of the fact that outside the wires life continued. A visit to another camp was an event: on Wednesday I shall go to the North Camp (that is across a gate) one said to oneself, as if one were going to cross to the continent; a visit to the theatre was a great event. To some people the walks outside the camp were events of importance, but I only took part in one. Between military guards you were marched along a muddy road with miners' cottages on either side. The streets were full of people, sneering or indifferent, and I thought that it made one realize the fact that one was a prisoner and degraded far more vividly than life behind the wires did, and so I never went again.

The very great events were, of course, the visits one received, looked forward to and remembered for many weeks. I do not remember how frequently one was allowed a visit, it may have been once a month or once every three months. I myself received a good many visits from one and only one friend who was not put off by the petty annoyances and troubles such a journey and a visit of that kind entailed to an Englishwoman. Such a visit was at the same time very exciting and infinitely depressing, and it was probably worse for the visitors than for the visited, for they felt and saw the changes prison life produced on their friends very much more than the prisoners themselves could notice them. What an unnecessarily gloomy performance it was! The visitors were placed on one side of a long table, then appeared their friends, husbands or brothers, heavily guarded as criminals, and sat down facing them. Officers in between, others wandering round, armed guards against the walls. Listeners all round you. Thus you were allowed 'conversation' during twenty-five minutes. Of course both sides had memorized all they wanted to say or ask many times and got through that in great haste. One must not speak of the war, one must not speak of the camp or the talk would be interrupted. And so it often happened that during half that short time, looked forward to for ages, one found nothing to say. Strange how hard it was to catch the sound of a woman's voice — most of the visitors were women — it seemed so unreal. Difficult to understand each other at all, people of different worlds. One tried to find out whether one still appeared fairly normal, for one no longer knew. One suddenly awoke to the fact that one was probably quite odd, that one had wandered far away, but one could not tell. A sign made by an officer, and it was all over. The visitors filed out, seemed unreal as soon as they had gone. Slowly and under escort one returned to camp.

There the others met one, the crowd that had had no visitors. They had stood pressed against the gates like caged animals, seen the visitors file past. Some had been mournful, some had made dirty jokes, now they all wanted news: When will the war be over? What do people think in London? — and one had no news to give them.

Often and often have I seen that procession pass by; some of the women were crying, some looked straight ahead, seeing nothing, some cast curious looks. As the years went on the visitors grew fewer in number. A good many men had foreign wives or fiancées, and not all of them remained true. There is one incident I remember, the last visit the wife of a friend of mine paid him with her little daughter. He was a young Rhenish engineer, his wife was French and he adored her, and still more the child, so he told me I must be sure to look out for them. I saw a pretty young woman and a little girl of six years or so pass, and in passing the child pointed its finger at the men behind the wires and said: '*Dis, maman, c'est ca les Boches?*' And shortly afterwards he told me she had left him and taken the child with her.

Of such nature were the visits, but between them one could read the diatribes of the papers against the thoughtless or criminal creatures who paid visits to the German prisoners, and dark hints about the scandalous scenes to be witnessed, and no one ever seemed to tell the public the truth.

These were the regular events recurring at more or less equal intervals, but all too often there were unforeseen events. All too often, for they were never of a pleasant nature; a surprise was bound to be a disagreeable surprise, because the history of the internment camps is one of measures growing ever more severe and of sudden catastrophes. All that misery can be summed up in the one word 'reprisals.' Germany had enforced some restriction,

England would adopt a similar one or one 'of equal value.' Each reproached the other with having 'begun first' like a couple of little boys; the prisoners on both sides were but pawns, the men who had to execute the orders but tools. As liberty was already restricted to the utmost and nearly everything interdicted anyway, there remained really only one field for punitive measures: food. One could write volumes about the importance food assumed under the circumstances. What was there for the vast majority of prisoners, torn from their work, their people, their interests, but sleep and meals? Food was their primary consideration from the start, but the scantier and the more unobtainable it became, the more it began to dominate all thought. Things became as I was to find them later on in half-famished Germany; people talked of nothing but food, thought of nothing else, and some tried by all means, fair or foul, to obtain more than was legally theirs.

This food problem did not, however, develop in a straight line, it passed through different phases. After the strict rationing of Knockaloe, Wakefield had seemed positively luxurious at first. As everyone paid, plenty could be bought; moreover, food parcels from England were allowed, and food parcels from Germany and Austria still very frequent. Had there been any sense of fairness left, it might have been thought that good and plentiful food, which the people, moreover, paid for was not too much to grant to people whose only crime was their nationality. But such considerations had disappeared long ago, prisoners were criminals and they were hostages as well. The press campaign against 'our pampered Huns' began to bear fruit, the credulous and unimaginative public protested against this crying scandal. Things began to get worse gradually, and complaints addressed to the 'Neutrals' supposed to look after these matters had no effect whatsoever.

It was all quite scientific. Vitamins had not yet been discovered; the scientific slogan of the times was 'calories.' Food had to contain a certain number of calories to keep people in a sufficient state of nourishment, and we were assured that we were receiving exactly the same number of calories as the prisoners in Germany. Whether these calories were contained in fresh meat and vegetables or in herring gone bad and frozen potatoes was apparently quite immaterial: that was not a scientific way of looking at it.

Things took a sudden and very decided turn for the worse after Germany had declared 'unrestricted submarine warfare.' Rationing began in England and rationing became very severe in the camps. There was now a justification for strict food economy, which the prisoners might have admitted if they had been less embittered. As it was, they considered, or professed to consider, the new restrictions as further proof of a policy of deliberate ill-treatment, and their mood became gloomier and more dissatisfied than ever. One article of diet after another vanished. Horseflesh made its appearance (it tastes like very tough and sugary beef), vegetables disappeared. Bread was gritty and mouldy, then it disappeared altogether for months and was replaced by 'broken biscuit' which is just like pebbles. Potatoes were frozen and sickeningly sweet, then there were no potatoes at all. Milk went, butter went. There was nothing now to be bought at the canteen and so one never got fruit. Every day or week made matters worse, until a time when one really always felt hungry. Everybody's health suffered and everybody's temper yet more. These privations do not sound so very terrible and there were certainly worse and greater hardships many had to bear in the world outside the wire. But it was not so much the actual want that made people miserable but their absolute helplessness; some anonymous power gave orders and these decided your fate. Bad as things were, they were sure to get worse, could only get worse. People got ever thinner, ever crosser, ever more listless, and they talked of, thought of, and lived for nothing but food.

It was then that commerce reverted to its primitive form of barter. Money became as good as useless, for people only wanted food, and that money could not buy. People hoarded and people bartered. If you still possessed two tins of sardines, you might exchange one for chocolate, half your bread ration might buy an apple. And as demands create supply, there appeared on the scene a number of barter-experts. They decided the value of the goods to be exchanged and their judgment was accepted as final. There was one little long-nosed man in our camp all went to when they could not agree amongst themselves. He was deaf and they shouted into his ear-trumpet: 'How many cigarettes ought he to give me for this piece of cheese?' The arbiter looked very wise and decided after a pause: 'Four cigarettes and a box of matches.' If anyone wanted to argue, he became stone deaf. So things were 'quoted' as on the stock exchange and their value fluctuated constantly. Only there was ever less to barter; parcels from friends in England had been forbidden long ago, visitors were no longer allowed to bring presents, and parcels from Germany and Austria had become very scarce, as rationing over there became extremely severe and prices for unrationed articles of food soared skywards. Sometimes one got quite a decent meal, more often one did not, and I shall never forget when one day my steward (there were a great many stewards by 1918) who always used the word 'we' brought my dinner with the remark, 'Today we have one potato for dinner, with tomato sauce.' One got very weak and one had to ration one's strength; if one wanted to do any work, the best thing was to lie still half the day and work steadily for a few hours. The winter from '17 to '18 was very hard, for one feels the cold very much more intensely when one is insufficiently nourished. The calories, in fact, refused to do the work their name implies. I suppose there was actually enough food given to the prisoners all the time if you adopt some sort of standard of weight or measurement without any regard to quality or composition. The German people were at the same time living under the same conditions: on rations declared sufficient by the experts, but in spite of the experts' decision the people suffered semi-starvation on both sides. And the worst part of such a state of affairs is not the actual privation but the degradation which nearly always results from it. It is easy to 'have a mind above food' when there is plenty to be had, but it is very difficult when it gets scarce and scanty. No one wants to be reminded of food after a plentiful meal, but after an insufficient one the thoughts continue to dwell on it. For more than a year after the war, until conditions improved gradually, Germany knew but one topic of conversation of supreme interest: food, and men or women of all classes thought of little else. Just the same happened in camp from 1917 on, and once people are reduced to that state the margin of difference between them and animals has become perilously narrow. In all probability the rumours of cases of cannibalism in certain remote corners of Germany, which were spread there during that period, were unfounded, but the fact alone that they had become believable shows the depths humanity had reached.

Hunger and fear of hunger was thus the great and ever-growing, disturbing menace. It was the great catastrophe which came on slowly, the minor disturbances, however, were sudden. All seemed to run comparatively smoothly and then something happened. There was an attempt of escape by prisoners in the North Camp for instance, which upset things badly for a time. Like everything in camp life it was both tragic and ludicrous. Some inhabitants of a hut standing quite near the wire had taken up the boards of the floor and started to dig a tunnel. Every night they removed the boards and went on with their slow underground work, and in the morning the boards were replaced. This went on for months without anyone knowing of it, and they had got well underneath the meadow outside the camp. They might have escaped from the camp, but for an unfortunate accident, though I don't know how they would have got out of the country. It rained hard for days and the rain loosened the soil, I suppose, and one day the ground gave way under a cow grazing on that meadow; the existence of the tunnel was revealed and it was traced back to the hut. But who were the culprits? For a short time people thought them heroes and their refusal to own up an excellent joke, but when all the camp or rather the three camps were punished by all manner of restrictions, people's temper changed rapidly, and the perpetrators of the deed were called fools and cowards. Then they owned up, or at least a sufficient number owned up; the camps once more were allowed visitors, parcels, etc., but very few had any sympathy with the unfortunate heroes and victims of this attempt for whom severe restrictions remained in force.

There was always fear of something happening; there were always rumours of unpleasant events; there was always suspicion of fraud. The kitchen management of the North Camp was found out cheating and vanished in a hurry, for the rule was to send such culprits to another camp; the chief captain of the West Camp disappeared for the same reasons. There was a horrible scene when one man was accused of denunciation, rightly or wrongly, I don't know, and crowds assembled to stone him before he could be removed. He was in hospital with wounds on his head for some days and then vanished into the unknown. There were terrible rumours about what was happening at the hospital; and what made all these rumours so terrifying was the impossibility of ever getting at the truth. The first story was this: the camp doctor and the German headman of the hospital had combined to prescribe injections for the patients which cost a lot of money; that was how they enriched themselves. Could it be true? Certainly lots of people got those injections; it is also a fact that the German headman was removed in a hurry and that the injections ceased. More one never learnt, but if it remained vague, it was quite enough to make one tremble at the thought of being ill. The second rumour arose later when a new doctor appeared. His methods were so exceedingly strange that people complained to the commandant, and that doctor again vanished in a hurry, apparently into an asylum. And every single story of that kind, always distorted and magnified by rumour, yet never entirely without basis, increased that atmosphere of distrust all round and the fear of trouble ever impending, though one never knew when a blow would fall or where it would come from.

Everyone's great aim was, as I have already explained at length, to get some sort of privacy by partitioning himself off, by building a cubicle. This was, I believe, never actually and expressly permitted, though it was silently tolerated. But there was no security. For months, perhaps a year, nothing would happen, and then there would be a new commandant, or someone else decided to interfere, and partitions would have to be lowered or destroyed altogether. Trifling, irritating vexations such things were, but they took on enormous proportions under the circumstances. The cubicle was a holy of holies, the one shred of individual existence and the proudest possession one had. To order its destruction was worse than ordering a man to destroy his house if he was at liberty and could build himself another. This uncertainty led to innumerable subterfuges; partitions were made to double up to half their height when inspection should come; lights — of which only a certain number were allowed, not enough to light all the cubicles — disappeared as if by magic, and even windows, to which the same rule applied, could be cleverly dissimulated. It was an incessant, embittered and schoolboyish campaign of deceit against a no less childish supervision. It seems almost too silly to write about, but it was of great importance at the time, for what is a trifling grievance under some conditions may be a stunning blow under others.

Some happenings there were that did not affect everyone but only a group of people. A young fellow died in hospital after a short illness; another went out of his mind; and these events plunged their friends into still deeper depression, while those who had not known the victims remained almost unaffected. Not entirely, because to all came the fleeting thought that they might meet a similar fate. How many more people would die there if that war went on and on; how many become insane? Sanity had, indeed, become a good deal more relative than it normally is, partly because the slight touch of insanity to be found in so many people remains their secret in normal life but becomes public property in camp, where nothing can escape detection, and partly because the strain had told on everybody's nerves and found expression in all manner of oddities. There were some who talked to themselves loudly as soon as they were alone; others who had to have their door opened for them for fear of meeting their double if they opened it themselves, or who never left their hut on certain days of the week, or, as in one case I knew, during autumn and winter. Such things were not discussed or argued but silently accepted and taken for granted, for no one could be sure how far he himself would still be considered perfectly sane and normal in the outside world: there was no standard of comparison to go by.

That it was not the mind or the reasoning power of the prisoners only which had become a little shaky, will be seen from an incident which happened to me and which in its absurdity verging on the tragic is extremely characteristic, I think. One day two guards appeared with the order to conduct me at once to the commandant. That only happened in extremely serious cases, for in all minor matters there was a complicated hierarchy which intervened between one and the supreme power. The whole camp got wildly excited and no doubt fantastic rumours spread during my absence. There had been no such agitation since some weeks earlier when a Zeppelin had thrown bombs in the near neighbourhood and the camp had been merged in darkness and fear. I myself could think of no possible explanation.

The commandant plunged straight into the heart of the matter. 'Your case is very serious indeed,' he addressed me, 'you have been carrying on a correspondence in cypher with the enemy.' I hadn't the slightest notion what he was talking about! The only letters I had written abroad were addressed to my mother and never even remotely alluded to the war. What could I possibly have had to tell her, even if I had wanted to, that would have been of any interest to anybody? And what on earth could he mean by a cypher? 'Surely there must be some mistake,' I said. He shook his head: 'No, no mistake possible. Do you recognize this as your writing?' He handed me two of my letters to my mother. 'Certainly,' I said. 'Then perhaps you can explain the meaning of these cypher-words,' he said and pointed to some words underlined by a censor's blue pencil. I read and the counter-climax was so great that I had great difficulty in repressing hysterical laughter. The words underlined were: *Der Golem*, *Meyrinck*, *Das grüne Gesicht*,[1] 'They are very easy to explain,' I said gravely, '*Meyrinck* is a famous author, and my mother sent me two novels of his, one called *Der Golem* and the other *Das grüne Gesicht*, for which I thanked her in one letter, while in the second I wrote that I had liked the first and did not think very much of the second.' The Commandant looked relieved; perhaps he would have got into trouble himself over this incident. 'Can you prove this?' he asked. 'I can prove it at once,' I replied, 'if you will send someone with me to whom I can give the two books.' He was really relieved now, and certainly I was. 'That should be a sufficient explanation,' he said, 'and I hope it will be accepted as such, for the authorities took an extremely serious view of the matter, let me tell you.' I was dismissed; a guard took the novels to the commandant, and that was the last I heard about it. But God knows what would have happened to me if I had written about books which I could not have produced! Such then were the happenings and events which interrupted monotony; they were varied enough, but they were invariably unpleasant,

---

1 German: The Green Face.

and one was thankful when the grey sameness one once had found it so hard to get accustomed to continued uninterrupted by any such upheavals.

Chapter XVI
A Change of Perspective

If you made a series of drawings of a place, a camp, for instance, from the usual angles, and then suddenly added an aerial view of it, the latter would certainly make the place look strikingly different, and anyone seeing it might not recognize it as the same place. Yet it would be the same place, and this example only illustrates the truth that things appear different according to the point of view taken. The application of this general truth to this book is this: that I have up till now described camp life as it appeared from one angle, and that in this chapter I propose to consider it from another, and that I feel this needs explaining. I have written of camp and camp life as it actually was, I have described it as objectively as I can — for there is no complete objectivity — and aimed at a picture of which those who have shared my experiences should say: 'Yes, that is what it was like,' and which could be accepted by the reader as the truth about the matter. That is what actually happened, that is how people lived, that is how the life affected them, and that is how they felt about it all, to the best of my knowledge. For that was my main object in writing this book at all: to show people what internment means, and leave them to draw their conclusions. That is why by far the greater part of the book is written from that angle, which I will call the objective and the general.

But there is another which I cannot neglect altogether: the subjective and the personal. If every prisoner were to give an account of his experiences, its first and general part should corroborate mine, but the second would be entirely different in each single case. To put the matter simply, the second part is concerned only with how the camp and its life affected one particular person; its subject is: what internment meant for me.

And here arises the danger of appearing contradictory, which I want to avoid. I have said what I consider the influence and results of internment life were according to my observations, and I have been objective in this; but the influence and results as far as I am concerned were of quite a different nature. This may be taken as an added proof of objectivity, for I certainly do not generalize from my own experience, which on the contrary I take to be quite exceptional, and that is why I wish to emphasize the fact that it must not be considered as contradicting the general truth. An influenza epidemic may result in one patient feeling better than he did before he fell ill, but that should not be taken to mean that an epidemic is to be recommended as a cure. I regard internment as horrible and as the cause of endless misery and major or minor tragedies, but to me personally it has been of the greatest value and assistance in spite of its horrors. It is not even enough to say, as so many people end by saying, after having expressed their horror of their war experiences: 'And yet I would not have missed it for anything'; it is not enough, because I cannot conceive myself at all as I am now without that experience. I should not be I, I should be a different I.

The years of internment mean an inner evolution in my case, for which the camp provided but the setting, and the outer events and circumstances but the background. That is what I mean by the simile of the view taken from above. Seen from the air barbed wire fencing, for instance, would not look much of a feature or an obstacle; and just so, from the point of view of my personal life in camp, all values are altered. Some things loom larger, others become insignificant, but the main point is that all outer things without exception become quite secondary. The outer possibilities were extremely limited and few, the inner were unlimited. During four years hardly anything happened, in the usual sense of the word, that I would have given much thought to under ordinary circumstances; but the life of the mind and the spirit became intensified as it would not have become if normal conditions had continued, for here life became to me one of contemplation and of thought. I speak for myself only and do not wish to generalize, but I would say that anyone inclined to thought and contemplation by nature must have found that tendency immensely strengthened by the enforced limitation of outer activity, or in more vulgar language: circumstances forced one to fall back on oneself.

Certain psychologists have brought the terms extraversion and introversion into use, and they may serve to explain my meaning. An extravert is a person who finds mental nourishment in the outside world, in other humans, in objects or events. He acts on them and they react on him, and his energy is turned outwards. An introvert, instead of pouring his mental energy outwards, turns it inwards, and the outer world, other humans, or events affect him only as far as they contribute to his inner development. The former will therefore need activity and change and be dependent on his surroundings, while the latter will incline to look on these as irrelevant to his main preoccupation. Needless to say, pure types do not exist; there is but a predominance of one tendency or the other, and when one gains the upper hand too completely mental equilibrium gets disturbed and the borders of sanity are reached. It stands to reason that most children of the world are strongly extraverted, that thinkers, philosophers, scientists, or strongly religious people tend to introversion, and that artists must combine both tendencies. Amongst artists, musicians are the most introverted, painters and sculptors the most extraverted, and writers hold an intermediate position. Applied to races one may say — very roughly, of course — that Europeans, men of the white race, are preponderantly extravert (the typical American is almost a pure extravert) while introversion is an Asiatic characteristic, which is why the Russians are the most introverted people of the white race.

This is rather a fascinating subject to go into, but I must leave it, for I only entered into it in order to explain that what happened to me in camp was a change from extraversion to introversion. My pre-war life had strengthened what extravert tendencies there were in me, my camp life awoke and strengthened all that was introvert, and the longer I remained there the more powerful that introversion became and the more indifferent to my surroundings did I come to feel. To a very great extent the camp, its conditions and hardships, ceased to affect me, and that is what I mean by a personal experience which has no general significance. Conditions were very trying, things were bad and getting worse, but they ceased to worry me, except when they interfered with what I was busy with. I was busy building up my own mind, gaining what the Germans call a *Weltanschauung*, that is, finding out what I thought of the world and of myself as related to it. Only I was not aware of all this at the time. There was no conscious effort, there never was a moment when I decided to devote my energies to the formation or enrichment of my personality, for that would have seemed very absurdly priggish to me. I am not a prig, I think, and I have a sense of the ridiculous which includes myself; on the other hand, I am lazy and very much of a fatalist, that is why

I would have been and still am quite incapable of a conscious effort to 'improve my mind.' What happened was simply that there were no outer interests left after a time, no activities of any significance, and that conditions and circumstances were best ignored. So my energies were turned inward.

There is no definite moment to which I can point and say: that is when the change began. It was a gradual change, so gradual that I was unaware of it, and it was often interrupted. It began, I should say, during the first winter, but I became aware of it only after I had found that all the varying ways in which I had continued to exercise my art had come to an end, that all that seemed void of significance to me, that painting, i.e., expression of emotion by means of pictorial representation, had become meaningless and that I had no desire for it, that something had died and something else taken its place. And that did not happen till three years later.

My chief interest before the war was art and all connected with it; I had always read a good deal, but without any particular purpose or system; I had all sorts of ideas on all sorts of subjects, but they were not coordinated in any way. Nor had I ever felt the need of any coordination except for fleeting moments; there was no time, one's thoughts were ever taken off by something new, and when I concentrated, it was on my painting. Quite instinctively I made an effort to continue my work in camp; was miserable when I found I could not work; continued to look for new possibilities. I was, without realising it, living on my past, working up what was still left over from it, and getting farther away from it all the time. I also read a good deal, as nearly everybody did, but it was not reading which originally turned my thoughts into new channels. It was spiritism.

I don't know where the impulse came from, but there were about seven or eight men, most of them friends of mine, who decided to try some experiments in spiritism. I had never been particularly interested in it, but I had an open mind on the matter, for I had always thought the so-called scientific attitude towards life quite stupidly limited, which I imagine every artist must feel if only because it quite fails to solve his problems or to account for art. I had even less patience with the limitations of the materialist orthodoxy than with those of religious orthodoxies, and it seemed to me that as truth had not yet been found anything might be true, and that as man, his senses and his intellect were very limited, it was very silly to deny the existence of things, beings, or worlds outside his ken offhand.

So why not try spiritism? It was at any rate something new and something to do. We decided to meet two or three times a week in a cubicle, shared by one of the men with two others, which had enough space, was comparatively quiet, and possessed the essential instrument of investigation into spiritism: a round table, for we had decided on 'table-turning.'

The practice is too well known to need description; it is slow and laborious, and the results we obtained were futile and discouraging. The table was certainly moved, often violently, by some sort of magnetism developed which one could not confuse with muscular effort, but when it came to slowly spelling out the messages its rapping conveyed the results were disappointing. Either they were senseless or else they could be traced to direct thought-transference. I tried the experiment of sitting in a corner away from the table and thinking hard of a word previously written on a piece of paper. Very frequently the table rapped out that word and thus thought-transference was proved. But though that was quite an interesting phenomenon, there seemed no particular point in going on proving it, nor any possibility of studying its mechanism. We all got father bored after a few months and gradually ceased the practice. A few weeks after this a curious incident happened. I was talking about our experiments with a man who thought them pure nonsense. He would not even admit that tables moved unless one helped them to, and pointed to a small square bamboo table standing near. 'Will you prove it by making this table move?' he asked. I explained to him that one always used wooden tables, round by preference, and that two people could hardly produce the necessary 'current.' That is why I did not think that the experiment could succeed, nor that its failure would prove anything whatsoever. But I saw no harm in trying. We had hardly sat down, with our hands touching, when the table got wildly agitated and started rapping out words in quick succession. The message, moreover, was quite clear. One fellow who had once or twice, but infrequently, taken part in our experiments, was to be told that his mother had died and that this message came from her. My friend at the table was astounded, but I was hardly less so. He was the man I have already alluded to, who developed religious mania later on, so he may quite possibly have been a strong medium without knowing it, which would explain the surprising success of that improbable experiment. Of course, we were both longing to find out whether that message contained a truth, but that was not quite easy. I did not know the man it was addressed to well, and I did not want to upset him by a message, the truth of which he could not verify for weeks, for letters often took several weeks to reach us. I was friends, however, with an intimate friend of his, from whom I first ascertained whether the man's mother was alive. He said she was, her son had heard from her and she was quite well. But a few weeks later he told me that the news of her death had arrived and that it must have taken place about the time we made our experiment.

Even in normal life this would have had its effect on me; in Wakefield it definitely turned my thoughts toward (what is called) the supernatural. It was, to say the least, an extraordinary case of thought-transference. Further than that I was not prepared to go, but that was strange enough. It did not lead me to any further experiments on the same lines, though I can hardly say why. Perhaps the reason is that I dislike the spiritists' conception of after-life, which I certainly do. I wanted other ways of approach to the occult, to the problem I was faced with, of how mind can act on matter, which is at the root of telepathy. What was matter, had it any real existence, was there a universal mind, did mind continue after death, were there other worlds, and what was this world and what was I in it? All these and many other related questions now began to absorb me. I had read some works on spiritism, amongst others Sir Oliver Lodge's *Raymond.*, which had just appeared. His theories about matter and mind seemed very plausible, though I could follow him no further. I determined to get as many works on occult phenomena as I could obtain, for there was no possibility of studying open to me except reading. In that manner I became acquainted with theosophy, which aroused my enthusiasm. For here there was much more than an explanation of one phenomenon or another; here there was a coherent, inclusive, and rational explanation of the universe and all its happenings. I felt as if I saw the world for the first time, as if absolute truth had been revealed to me. I read most of the works of that most extraordinary woman, Mrs. Annie Besant, whom I still consider one of the greatest personalities of our times, though I have long ceased to believe in her teachings; and they led me to the study of her predecessor, Helena Blavatsky. Blavatsky's books are as fantastic as her life. A prophet to some, an impostor to others, and probably something of both, she was most certainly a genius. Her works, her cosmogonies are as superb as they are chaotic and obscure, and if she is an impostor and did not obtain her 'secret doctrine' from the mystical sources she ascribed them to, she should be classed with William Blake as a mystic poet of unsurpassed power. But also, as I went on reading, I found more and more contradictory doctrines and messages, all professing to continue the only true theosophical tradition, chief of which was the 'Anthroposophy' of Rudolf Steiner, which has very many followers on the continent. He tries to combine more purely

Christian tradition and beliefs with the Indian ones of the original theosophists, and their warfare is bitter indeed.

I had many discussions with three or four friends whom my enthusiasm had infected, and there were at least as many opinions as people. This could get me no farther, and so I decided to go back to where the theosophists had got their inspiration from: to the sacred books of India. I read and read. I got to know some of the most magnificent books humanity has produced, amongst which I count the *Bhagavad Gita*. One could perhaps deduce from them what the theosophists have deduced, but there were many different ways of explaining their doctrines, for they are as a tropical jungle and not like the rational and ordered theosophical system derived from them, just as innumerable other sects and movements have had their origin in them.

I read Chinese mystics and confronted Lao-Tse with the anti-mystic Kon-fu-tse,[1] I read Sufi poetry, I read what one could get of the Cabbalists. I read European philosophers, of whom Schopenhauer and Bergson seemed most akin to and aware of Eastern wisdom; I read many of the minor lights. They all seemed to me to agree on the essential truths of a Universe spiritual in character, animated by a Universal spirit, of which the material world our senses show us is but an image. But the more I read them, the more closer investigation, which must necessarily be carried out by material means, faded out of the reach of possibility. If there was truth, it was revealed in mystic contemplation, and the truth revealed to the Christian saint was of Christian inspiration and that of the Hindu remained Hindu, and in the end it came to what it had been before I set out on that voyage of discovery: a question of belief, as soon as you transcended the narrow limits of human reason. These were things beyond the intellect, to be approached by contemplation, by meditation — and how was one

---

[1] Commonly known in English as Confucius.

to meditate or contemplate when it was impossible to be alone and undisturbed by noise and movement?

But what was that part of one's spirit outside intellect that could be trained to a larger perception? It was when pondering this somewhat paradoxical problem — for how could one hope that one's intellect would understand faculties beyond it? — that I came across the works of Freud, which my friend the medical student pressed upon me. I began to read them with great reluctance, for they seemed like a sudden cold shower. This was the very opposite way of approach to the one I had taken. That world had been all spirit, this one was all sex. But, as I continued, I could not shut my eyes to the truths contained in Freud's teachings. I would have liked to, for they seemed to destroy the conception of the Universe I had so laboriously arrived at, but I could not, for they confirmed too many of my own experiences. Also they explained much of what had puzzled me in the confused complexity of the teachings and lives of theosophists and mystics. Psychoanalysis was, in fact, the necessary corrective to mysticism, it was another half-truth. The one began up in the clouds and refused to descend to the ground; the other began deep below ground and denied the skies, but yet I felt that they were not contradictory but complementary, in that both recognized the preponderance of the irrational, of the instinctive, the intuitive as the others called it, over the purely reasonable. Reason, intellect, normal consciousness, were but part of one's spiritual whole, and could only take in part of the Universe. Particularly the writings of Jung and the Zürich school satisfied me, for while starting on the premises of the Freudians they went beyond them, and while accepting the truth that all could be reduced, analysed back to the sexual, they were more preoccupied with the sublimation, the building up of that spiritual material. While acknowledging the underground origins, they did not deny or ignore the skies. Thus the circle was closed after a manner. If I had not solved the riddles of the Universe, of human personality, and of matter and spirit, I felt that I had at least gained a point of vantage from which to consider them. If much remained mysterious and unknowable, it was no longer chaotic and confused. I was at that time re-reading Goethe's talks with Eckermann, a book which contains more wisdom than any other work of modern times, and I accepted Goethe's verdict: 'Man must recognize the frontiers of the unknowable and respect them,' just as I thought that when he talked of all his work as being no more than a symbol, and of the Universe as a parable, I found him confirming what all the sages of the East had said. We must recognize that an immensity lies beyond our intellectual comprehension, and that what we can comprehend is but an image, but we are foolish if we attempt to make our reason do what it is not fit for. Or as Schopenhauer puts it paradoxically: 'I am convinced of the truth of mysticism, but I distrust the experiences of all mystics.'

Chapter XVII
The End of the World

The years of internment, the physical privations were having their effect on me as on everybody. I felt rather weak, I had got very thin, I had to rest a good deal if I wanted to get any work done. But there were compensations, for one's sensibility seemed to increase with the decrease of one's physical strength. I began to understand why fasting plays so great a part in church discipline. Everything in this world has to be paid for, and robust health and psychic development do not go together. Just as the monotony of outward life was compensated by an increase of spiritual activity, so a weakening physique was compensated by what I believe to have been a strengthening of inner perception, an awareness of what one is normally too gross, too dense to become aware of.

I began to dream a great deal at that time, and extraordinarily vividly. There were many dreams influenced by my readings, and those which appeared after reading psycho-analytical books served to convince me that one cannot take dreams as proofs of the truth of a theory, which is their cause in many cases. I had one dream which was very illuminating. It was winter once more, the third winter in camp, it was cold and dark, the evenings seemed endless in the vitiated air of the hut. The end of the war seemed farther away than ever; I was always cold, and felt as if I had very little vitality left. How indescribably happy one would have been if one had had a room to oneself, properly heated and comfortable! So I thought, and then came my dream. I was standing in front of a palace of white marble, built round a circular court like that of Charles V's palace inside the Alhambra. The entrance was guarded, somewhat incongruously, by three men in shabby evening dress, sitting behind a counter covered in red, such as guard — God knows why — the entrance to Paris theatres and scribble something in blue pencil on a piece of paper they hand you. Also I knew, as one knows things in dreams, that this was the privileged camp of Douglas. The palace was magnificent, the sun shone, the sea stretched blue behind the white marble; everything was heavenly. What I said was: 'Has my room been reserved for me?' One of the men handed me a blue-pencilled ticket and pointed to a window facing the pillared court. 'Up there,' he said. And I was extremely angry. 'I am not going to take a room without a sea view under any circumstances whatsoever,' I heard myself say grandly, and with that awoke. I also awoke to the realization that I had to acquired far less wisdom than I imagined, that I had really, like the Bourbons, learnt nothing and forgotten nothing. My subconscious had remained unaltered.

That is what these dreams were: strange warnings of the subconscious to normal consciousness, dialogues between part of myself with another unrealized part, which knew far more about myself than I knew. Call it the subconscious and it sounds 'reasonable' enough for everyone to accept the explanation — quite scientific in fact. But is it certain that that subconscious is an individual possession? Or is it something far larger, far deeper, and far more mysterious?

The dream I will describe now was the last of my dreams, and I relate it without offering an explanation. I awoke one night or dreamt that I awoke, I do not know which. Before me was a picture of the kind I have called my imaginative drawings, a very few of which, connected with my metaphysical searchings, I had done in the last year. This was a triptych, both larger and far more elaborate than anything I had done, and there were many figures in it. The centre was a fantastic walled city crowned by a monstrous head, two more monstrous shapes were in the yellow sky, and before the city was the crucified figure of a man. Some of the figures bore faces of people known to me in the camp, but the majority were figures which belonged to former drawings of mine, to my pre-war life. The picture was clear in every detail and I examined it a long time; it was an extract and a conclusion of what my life and my work had been for perhaps the last ten years. And I knew, as one knows in dreams, that is without hearing or seeing, that the picture was called: '*La fin d'un monde*' (not '*La fin du monde*,*'* that was quite clear), and as even my dreams seem to be polyglot I heard a deep voice saying: '*Dies ist Dein letztes Bild*' (This is your last picture). Then I awoke or dreamt that I awoke with a loud cry which no one seems to have heard.

I remained dazed by the dream for quite a time. I have purposely mentioned the state of my health, so as to give an opportunity for the usual explanations: in a state of lowered vitality, possibly of feverishness; in a 'barbed wire' state in short; visionary or auditory hallucinations are quite common, and there is nothing very surprising, still less anything supernatural in this experience. Well, perhaps. But the dream had terrified me, for I was convinced that my death was near at hand, nor did I feel that to be at all improbable. And so, childishly, I wanted to cheat fate, and I did not begin that work for weeks. But I could not get it out of my head, it pursued me, and so at last I resigned myself to fate, began the work, and finished it lingeringly in about six weeks. And nothing happened. I felt neither worse nor better than before....

I had not interrupted my reading and studies altogether, but after that spell of pictorial work I took them up again with renewed enthusiasm. For quite a time already it had become my habit to make extracts from the books I read, and to compare these extracts. The next step was to write down my commentaries on extracts and books, the commentaries swelled into essays, and almost without being aware of what I had undertaken I found myself engaged in writing a book on the evolution of the arts. This contained the expression of my convictions about art as they had been formed by my studies; I wrote about the place of art in the general scheme of things, its importance in evolution, and on the evolution of art itself and of its different branches. This my first book has never been published and I lost the MS. with the exception of a few pages. I wrote it very quickly, I remember; it almost seemed to write itself. Immediately after I began another book called *The Mission of the Jew*, trying to define the Jews' position and import in the world as they seemed to me. I wrote it in English and a friend of mine who was enthusiastic about it sent it to different prominent English Jews. They wrote flattering letters about it, though each one of them disagreed with my views, the orthodox considering me too liberal, the Zionists not sufficiently aware of the fact that there was a Jewish nation, and too preoccupied with the religious aspect, etc. There was only one thing they all agreed about and that was the impossibility of publishing it while the war lasted. It was eventually published in Germany, as my second book to appear, and while the first had found an extraordinarily good reception, this one pleased nobody. The country was in feverish unrest, the Jewish public thought any discussion of their problems inadvisable, the others were not interested.

Amusingly enough, the few letters of approval I received came from Catholic and Protestant clergymen. Incidentally, I found translating my own work from one language into another very difficult and very tiresome. I have translated the work of a good many other people and consider all these translations far superior to that of my own. My only other work of the same kind has been the translation of a prose-poem I wrote in German into English, and that seemed much easier. In Germany this appeared in an *édition de luxe*, in England in the review *The Quest*. It was called *The Smile of the Seven Buddhas*, and though written in 1920 is still, as I now realize, a fruit of Wakefield. The chief result of what I consider my spiritual education at Wakefield was, however, my first book to be published (in 1920). To a great extent I had written it in camp, but when I left camp I was not allowed to take any writings of any sort, not even a piece of paper with me. Some of my writings left behind (like the MS. of *The Mission of the Jew*) were preserved and I got them about a year or so later, but a great many had gone. But in any case I would not wait, so I wrote my book all over again and it appeared in 1920. Its title is *Asien als Erzieher*, which one might translate as *The Message of Asia*, and it consists of a series of eighteen essays on all the problems which had been uppermost in my mind during the war years. While I have changed my opinions about several of these questions since that time, and have, I am sorry to say, become less of an optimist, I still regard it as the basis of all I have written since.

This then was my transformation during and by prison life: from a painter I had become a writer, and one day I remembered my dream and sat up with a start. That drawing *had* been my last drawing! Though I was not aware of it at the time, the *fin d'un monde*, the end of one world, had come about, and that was its summing-up and a farewell to it.

A new world had begun and it was expressing itself in writing. When, after a long while, I began to paint again, my work no longer resembled the former work in the least, and nobody not familiar with the two has ever attributed them to one and the same painter. These new watercolours were of sea and sky, very slight and extremely simple. As near a representation of empty space and atmosphere as one could get. Formerly all had been filled to overflowing with symbols and signs of confused thought and emotion, now all that had flowed into more purely intellectual channels, confusion had become order and ordered thought expressed itself in writing. All that was left over for painting was my love of colour, of subdued colour now, and perhaps a certain lyrical tendency, but it cannot have been a very powerful impulse for it died down after some years. People who know my former work often ask me why I never paint now and I can only reply that I have no desire to paint anymore. I have nothing to say, nothing new to express, I see no object in repeating oneself and I have never wished to manufacture pictorial souvenirs. Wakefield brought me the death of one thing, the birth of another, its importance to me has been vital. Compared with this aspect all its others fade into complete insignificance as far as I am concerned, and, of course, only as far as I am concerned. I cannot call this bad or good, for it has become part of myself.

Chapter XVIII
The Scene Shifts

About Christmas 1917, I achieved a most cherished ambition; I got a cubicle to myself. This meant leaving one hut for another, a resolution which sounds easy but was very difficult in the circumstances, because any change meant a great effort, because each hut had become almost a separate territory, but chief of all because the year-long habit of having everything decided for one had made one almost incapable of taking any decision. However, I managed to take the great step and I certainly never regretted having taken it. No one can imagine what it means to be able to shut oneself in alone between four walls, even if they are matchboard walls, unless he has had to do altogether without privacy for years. Being alone with the certitude that no one would come in without knocking at the door first was heavenly. One still heard all the noise around, but one felt it did not concern one, it was a rest-cure for one's nerves.

It is remarkable how little can make one happy when one has had less — my 'room' measured six feet by four, the size of a large bed. That was the space allotted to one man, and I got so used to it that for years I could not see a room without mentally calculating how many prisoners it would hold, how many cubicles one could construct in it. It was very difficult to achieve such single bliss, for so many things had to coincide: one had to be able to get wood, which was not the case very often, and furthermore a permit for this was indispensable, and then the space had to be available and that depended on other people's dispositions. Now all these factors combined at last, and so building began. The chief difficulty was that a window had to be put in, which was severely prohibited, but quite a technique to be employed in such cases had developed. The window was first completed in the 'carpenter's shop'; then one had to wait for a fine day, when rugs were normally hung out to dry between the huts, for this prevented the guards outside the wires from seeing the walls of the hut. Then the sawing began and all gramophones were turned on and instruments played to cover the noise. The whole work took no more than a quarter of an hour, but that was one of breathless excitement. Once a window was put in, everyone was prepared to swear it had always been there, but none of these additions were ever noticed. The next indispensable contrivance was very ingenious as well. One was allowed an oil lamp if one was the happy owner of a single cell because it had to be lighted and there must be no new electric lights; but one had to put it out when the lights-out signal was given, and the guards saw any light left on. So a frame had to be evolved which fitted tightly into the window; it was covered with cardboard, and not even a shimmer could be detected from outside. This meant being able to sit up or read in bed, another marvellous improvement. I was less lucky about the heating, for though I had got the permission to acquire an oil stove I could get no oil for it for three or four weeks, the little oil available being needed for my lamp.

It was a marvellous place, my cubicle. If I had not seen it, I should never believe what six feet by four can be made to hold.

There was a bed on the sleeping-car system, which went up against the wall in daytime, when a curtain hid it, and a couch, which was a box with cushions on it, was revealed underneath it. The curtain also hid washing-basin and like paraphernalia. Above the bed was a long shelf for books, quite a library, before the window a small collapsible table (again on sleeping-car principles), and along the other long wall a cupboard for clothes and belongings, only a few inches deep but six feet long. There were furthermore two tiny tabourets, vestiges of my stage activity, and a deckchair which could be hidden behind the curtain. But that cubicle was not only practical but handsome as well. The walls were papered in grey-blue, the woodwork was stained brown, the curtain was an Indian print, a red silk handkerchief made a lampshade, and there were paintings on the wall where any space remained. It seemed a superb decorative effort and I was very proud of it and very happy in its possession. What a way to have travelled since the *paillasse* of the first night, even if it had taken three years and a half!

I settled down to enjoy this new luxury and comfort, and my happiest time in camp began. If I felt pretty weak, I was of greater mental lucidity than ever before (or after), and one thing compensated for the other. I had embarked on my new career of writing, of expressing what seemed to me the truth about all the problems I had pondered over, and I could now have the necessary quietude for working. I was in addition running my 'theatre club' and so pleasing others. Contrary to my principle of never laying in provisions, in spite of all alarms, I had bought a little stock of soap when it was announced that that article too was going to vanish, and provided with soap, oil (which I obtained in January), a cubicle and great works to be done I was facing the future more cheerfully than at any time since August 1914.

No outer events disturbed me, except once when I was told to go and be examined by the doctor, for which I could find no reason. I was weighed, examined, asked all sorts of questions, and

I assured him most untruthfully that I had never felt so well and physically fit in all my life, for I was desperately afraid of being sent to the hospital. But I was dismissed, and as nothing further happened I classed this with the many incomprehensible happenings and commands of camp existence, and forgot all about it. I had but one wish, to be left alone, and that wish was being fulfilled now at last. I had, it seemed to me, surmounted all prison troubles, and was going to be quite happy and contented there for any length of time.

It was early in February, a week, perhaps, after I had reached that state of complete bliss, that I was ordered to appear before the commandant and told that I was going to be sent to Holland. For nearly a year, I think, a plan had been discussed for an exchange of prisoners in England and in Germany, whose health was bad. An equal number of both military and civilian prisoners were to be interned in Holland. I had read about this plan, but it never seemed to materialize and I had long forgotten all about it. Now it had suddenly become a fact and about a dozen prisoners from Wakefield were on the first list of transfer just published. My name was among them, and to this day I do not know how it got there, but there it was.

Like all others I had often and often wondered how and in what manner internment would come to an end. When the newspapers were rolled in on a barrow each day, I thought that one day the first man to open one — and what a rush there always was to be the first — would shout: 'Peace! Peace is declared!' for surely it must happen someday, and where should one be then except in Wakefield. Would they let one go at once, would there be more transports? They might be extremely unpleasant about it or there might be a sort of general handshaking, no one could tell. But the one thing I had never contemplated was another change, and the one eventuality I should have thought impossible was that when my release came I could be anything but overjoyed. And now I was to leave within twenty-four hours, the very next morning, and all I felt was profound anxiety. I was not only not overjoyed, not only not pleased, I was thoroughly miserable and frightened. I felt that I had been cheated out of the fruit of all my efforts. And now a new and great effort was demanded of me and I felt quite incapable of it.

The camp was in a ferment of excitement, hundreds of people congratulated me, all thought that their turn might soon come now. I felt absolutely dazed, incapable of thought or action. I could not grasp or believe in this change. Moving from one hut to the next had meant a great strain on one's energy, moving into another camp had long become too great an effort for anybody to attempt, going out into something absolutely unknown was too much to demand from human nature, I felt. Leave my cubicle, my friends, my theatre, my work, all that existence built up by the efforts of years — it seemed unbearable. I just could not do it, I did not want this, I hated it, I wanted to be left alone. This was just as bad as being torn out of one's life to be interned years ago, ages ago, in another life it seemed to have been. It was worse. One was just as helpless, one was just as much of a parcel to be bundled off, but one was worn out, feeble, incapable of effort. One had vaguely looked forward to an end that would come someday, but never to a new situation other than peace. What was this new thing, what was 'being interned in Holland'? Why on earth should anyone wish to go and be interned somewhere else? Why on earth did they all congratulate me? I could see no reason for it at all. A neutral country, they said — well, what of that? This country did not bother me, I did not care what uniform the guards wore. Would Dutch barbed wire look any different? Decent food, yes, that was not to be despised; but, against that, no cubicle, no friends, no books — a sort of Knockaloe on its first day again. No, that was nonsense, it would be much better, of course! Perhaps one would not really be interned again at all. It was awful all the same.

I began to pack, to unpack, to dismantle; all was confusion. Some friends helped me. The orders were out: nothing but clothing and personal effects were allowed to be taken, all other things could be sent to any address in England; they were to be packed and given up with the keys by 5 p.m. Not a piece of paper of any sort whatsoever was to be taken, and there would be a rigorous search. That was, I suppose, to prevent any communications that might be dangerous. It meant leaving even one's passport and all papers of identification behind, and to me it meant leaving behind all my MSS., my many notes, my books, my drawings and paintings, all my work and all means of continuing it, except my memory. It was a true catastrophe.

I had two boxes, two pieces of hand baggage. The box I was to take was easy to pack, but the other could not hold half of what I had to leave behind. I packed and unpacked, I gave away half my books, I sold all my furnishings (the 'expert' did that for me), ruefully I gave away my soap (I should not have laid in even that provision — that was what had come of it!), my few tins, God knows what else. The second box consented to shut at last; that was over and I felt as if I had buried myself. All that was essential lay in that box, all I had left were some clothes. The box was carried out, like a coffin.

People came, people went; I have no clear memory of anything that happened before my departure. One shook hands, one agreed mechanically that one was lucky indeed. Of course, all the others would follow — soon now. Yes, it was the beginning of the end, it was only being done because peace was about to be concluded. One said goodbye to one's friends, of course one would write often, every week — did one not know what letters meant. One would write to their people and tell them exactly how things really were — no, one would not forget. And parcels, of course, through the Red Cross which alone was allowed to send them. No, one could not write down their people's address and take it, they must write it when one was there. There? Where? Well no, one would write first and give one's address to them and then they would write. Yes, that would take a long time, but I would not forget. Really I would not forget. Yes, I was indeed lucky. My head went round in a whirl, I felt dead tired, too tired to think or to feel any emotion of any sort.

No, I would not forget...

Chapter XIX
Interlude

I have always admired the people whose emotions and feelings at crucial moments are so clear-cut and defined that they can describe them graphically later on, but my admiration contains an admixture of incredulity because my own experience is so different. I find that when I am faced with sudden tragedy or disaster, with a great change or, indeed, any event which should arouse very strong emotion, I feel none at all. That comes later or it may have been exhausted before, but at the actual moment all seems a dream and not even as vivid as some dreams. Things seem to be happening to someone else, not to myself, and I simply feel rather dazed and quite indifferent. That is how I had felt on the first day of my imprisonment when faced by that East End mob and that is how I felt when the barbed wire gates of Wakefield opened before me. Neither regret nor joy, just vague wonder at my own indifference. Crowds, amongst which were my friends, stood pressed against the wires of the West and the South Camps, between which ran the road to the outer world, to watch this exodus, but I do not remember recognizing any face or paying much attention to them. Then the great gate closed behind me, but it did not impress me more than any casually closed door. We must have been about eight prisoners and two or three guards, and we took a tram which runs down a steep hill to Wakefield Station. It was then that a very simple incident suddenly roused me: the conductor demanded his fare from me.

I stared at him as if he had asked me to fly. It was too wildly improbable, and such things did not happen. What did he think I was, an independent human being responsible for his movements? I was part of a transport, I was number 1972, I had no permit for this payment, his demand was preposterous in its ignorance. 'Fares please,' he repeated, and I looked around at the guards behind, but they did not seem to see anything remarkable in the proceedings. So I handed him sixpence and he gave me the change, but I had not recovered from my uneasiness when we got out at the station.

The journey was full of surprises to me. There was a long wait for the train and in the waiting room one man was bold enough to ask if one was allowed to have a drink. Not only was one allowed this, but one was allowed to stand the guards drinks, and the barmaid — a real barmaid of the female sex with an odd, high-pitched voice — did not seem to feel how extraordinary all this was, but said her 'Two shillings please' and her 'Your change' without the slightest trace of emotion, without visible signs of hostility or fear. Then the train came and it was an ordinary train, just some compartments reserved for us and the guards. Some passengers looked out of the windows, but they again seemed to see no brand of Cain on us, and remained quite indifferent. So the train started on its journey into the unknown.

All I knew was that we were going to Boston, a place I had never seen, for it had been agreed that the hospital ships which were to convey the prisoners to Holland should start from there.

I thought that the train would run straight up to the steamer, or, rather, I did not think about it at all. I suppose that subconsciously I expected the usual pre-war voyage to Holland: one went on board in the evening and woke there early next morning, feeling very sick as a rule. I don't remember how long we were in that train, it was marvellously comfortable and the seats the first sample of the art of upholstery I had encountered for nearly four years — quite long enough to forget that such things could be. I slept some of the time; I looked out of the window and felt happy in a somnolent way.

I would have liked that journey to continue for weeks, but it came to a stop all too soon. We stood shivering on a railway platform, it was getting dark, it was snowing. New guards came, luggage was piled on a cart, we were marched off. It seemed a bit of a comedown after that *train de luxe* existence, but far more natural. We were being marched to the hospital ship, I thought. Hospital ship sounded rather alarming; I did not feel like an invalid and did not want nurses and doctors, yet it might be quite comfortable and, at any rate, it was sure to be well-heated. I should lie down at once, I felt quite tired enough, then the steamer would hoot and glide out — and one would awake in 'a neutral country.' After that — well, it was no use bothering one's head about what might happen then.

It seems to have been written in the stars that during all my captivity everything should turn out contrary to my expectations. Stratford-on-Avon became Stratford, East London, Knockaloe had come as a pleasant surprise, Wakefield which was to be a paradise had seemed more like the other place for months, then after years it had come to seem almost a perfect abode for me — no matter what a hell it might be to others — and at that moment I had been forced to leave it, and now when I thought I had arrived at the end of my prison experiences in England, when I felt the latter time compensated the former, when I was expecting a night in a hospital ship, I was led into the courtyard of a prison.

To be quite exact, it was not a prison, it was a workhouse, but that subtle distinction quite failed to comfort me. It already contained a good many prisoners who had been brought there from other camps, and I soon learned what had happened. There was a positive part to what they had to relate and a conjectural one. The positive part was told in a few words, but they were formidable enough: the exchange of prisoners to Holland had been stopped. The conjectural one was extensive, it told me the reasons of the stoppage and its consequences. Naturally it consisted of rumours, those ceaseless, horrible and menacing rumours which ever poisoned camp life, and as usual the rumours were contradictory. There was a tale that the first hospital ship had run on a mine, another that the Germans had insisted on a change of port of departure, a third that the English had not sent the agreed number of prisoners, though some knew that it was the Germans who had not sent enough men. Some others swore that the numbers had been correct, but that some important personages had been retained, others again that the stoppage was a 'reprisal' for some action not connected with the exchange at all, while the most pessimistic had it on good authority that the scheme was definitely dropped because the Dutch Government had changed its mind and refused to take on that responsibility. As to the future there were quite as many and varying versions: this only meant an interruption of one day according to some, of weeks, months or a definite one according to others. We would all be imprisoned here indefinitely, we would all be returned to our camps, we would all be sent to the Isle of Man.

Everyone talked, everyone guessed, everyone was horribly depressed. Whatever the future might bring, this present disappointment was too great, the present surroundings too sinister. It must be remembered that all the people there had been chosen on account of their bad health and that there were really few amongst them fit to face new privations and discomforts. It was a truly terrible situation and all the more terrible because it had been so unexpected. Its chief horror was again uncertainty; for it is worse to be imprisoned for an uncertain length of time than for a determined length, even if the latter should be long and the former turn out to have been short. Beside that central fact there were quite enough others to make one feel pretty desperate. I felt I had come back where I started: this was Stratford all over again, a little better in some respects, much worse in others. It was a big, bare, stone building and horribly cold. One slept in dormitories which were unheated, wrapped up in all one could find; everything was as cheerless and comfortless as it had been on the first day of that life. It was worse in some ways, for one had not a book to read nor could one write. One only had one's clothes. There was no organization of any sort, for this had not been foreseen; there was no canteen at all at first, though on the second day one could obtain a few things. There was a small courtyard closed in by buildings to walk about in, and there was literally nothing one could do but watch the aeroplanes buzzing about in the skies all day, for apparently there was an aviation camp or school close by. Altogether, it was quite the worst time I spent as a prisoner, as well as the most irritating. I had one pleasant surprise, which was seeing Dr. A., the anarchist agitator of my first Knockaloe days again. He looked wilder than ever, though considerably more clothed on account of the cold, and he was quite furious because he was amongst the men, of whom there were quite a number at this place, who were to be sent back to Germany in exchange for English prisoners. This was the last thing he desired as he expected a very warm reception there. I imagine he was a deserter, but he may have been wanted for political offences, at any rate he told me that he was determined not to return to Germany. I don't know how he managed it, but when, after arrival in Holland, the roll call was taken he was missing. I met him some months later and he told me that Dutch friends of his had helped him; that was the last time I saw him, but I read about him in 1919: he was then leader of a group of anarchists who had decided to live *en plein air* somewhere in the woods near Berlin, and the police were after them. They were caught, and he was accused of and condemned for offences against the law, illegal medicinal practices committed before the war. Meanwhile at Boston we exchanged experiences. I told him of mine, which he disapproved of, being a convinced materialist, and he told me of his, which were of the higher mathematical variety and which remained enigmatic to me. Even the simplest mathematics have always seemed utterly incomprehensible to me, and I have never been able to understand why anyone should care what happens to x and y or π; he assured me, however, that I had really arrived at the same conclusions as he had, though in a confused manner, whereas he could sum up all the world and its workings in one simple mathematical formula which he kept shouting at me. So I left it at that.

I cannot say at all how long I shivered in that workhouse. I have explained how one had come to lose all notion of time, and at Boston there was absolutely nothing to distinguish one day from another. To me it seemed months, every day seemed interminable, in fact, but I imagine that according to normal measurements it was somewhere between a week and a fortnight. Then we were told in the evening that we should be leaving early next morning.

We actually did. It was quite a long way to the steamer. When we had arrived, a cart had transported all luggage, but this time we had to carry all hand baggage, and when men found it getting too heavy, they simply had to leave it standing in the road. I have never seen anything more forlorn-looking than those bundles, packages, and valises in the snow by the roadside. There were a good many, for most men were not strong enough to carry what they had set out with; fortunately, my load was light. This was like a last symbol of the system in its senseless waste and needless hardness. We reached the ship at last and went on board. The luggage arrived, the boxes were thrown on board and some of them fell into the water and were lost, which the porters thought quite a good joke. The steamer hooted, it began slowly to move. We were leaving England. I could not believe it, though. We were steaming up a narrow waterway and a very lovely church tower appeared and grew as we moved on; the 'Boston stump' I thought, the one that St. Dunstan's in Fleet Street is copied from. I must have a look at it when I pass Fleet Street. Then I remembered, and then again all seemed incredible. Those low marshes looked as they had always looked, there were cottages and people in them, there were cattle in the fields, the world was as it always had been. Was war real, were people really killing each other now, had they been killing each other for four years? Were there really others locked up in cages of barbed wire, turning round and round in them, and had I been one of them, or was it all a bad dream? And where and to what was this ship gliding?

Chapter XX
The Last Phase

It was a strange voyage and it seemed endless. Fortunately the sea was quite calm, for I am a bad sailor and think seasickness one of the worst evils. All day long we kept near the coast, all other shipping apparently did the same. There was a great deal of it, and it looked very odd, nearly all steamers being 'camouflaged', which made them look as if cubist painters had been busy on them or natives of Africa had done their worst; it also made them look curiously decrepit as they crawled along as slowly as we did ourselves. We also saw a convoy or two, all in dark grey paint and suggestive of a funeral. We were presented with lifebelts or jackets and shown how to put them on, which made all one had read about mines and submarines seem very vivid. At night we anchored somewhere near the coast, I do not know where, and one had to go below deck.

I need not have worried about doctors and nurses, for if there were any I certainly never saw them or anybody else at all anxious about one's state of health. Why this steamer was labelled a hospital ship I cannot imagine; it was just like the steamers which ran between England and Holland in the days of peace. The only difference was that there were far too many passengers on board and that people slept all over the place. The next day the voyage continued. I suppose that for some reason or other it lasted much longer than had been supposed, because food became very scanty and washing water was at a premium, which was worse. I think it was the second night we reached Holland, possibly it was the third, it seemed about the tenth, for voyages have that in common with prison life that one loses count of time, and this was a combination of the two. We were to land at Rotterdam eventually, but that night we anchored at the Hook and so there was one more night to be passed on board before one could know one's future fate.

I knew hardly any of my fellow passengers except the few that had come with me from Wakefield. The majority were to go on to Germany in exchange for British prisoners, the others were to stay in Holland. It was a curiously subdued crowd, and all that voyage has remained in my memory as something silent and ghostly and grey. Grey waters and sky, a lifeless sea, a creeping steamer and grey and tired-looking, silent men on it. One felt one ought to talk in whispers. On that first evening nothing happened at all; one stood about on deck and gazed at a deserted quay and all seemed dead, but in the early morning the boat began to move on and soon reached Rotterdam, or at least a remote quay with a station building on it.

There was no joyous reception awaiting us; there was, in fact, no one to receive us at all. On this side of the water things were exactly the same as on the other, and this was the first evidence. Neither the Dutch nor the German authorities had been warned in time of our coming, it appeared, and as most of them had to come from the Hague, several hours passed before they arrived. It was then discovered that they were not expecting exchange-prisoners at all, but a batch of women and children, and so all arrangements had to be modified. In the meantime they held a roll call and found all correct except that one man — the famous revolutionary doctor — had disappeared. When I say that they found all correct I must qualify this statement. The lists were found correct, the men inscribed on them all but one answered to their names when called, and it was easy to sort those to go on to Germany from those to stay on in Holland. But this did not satisfy the authorities at all, for what was there to prove that these people were really what they pretended to be? There was nothing, and they looked on each one of us with the greatest suspicion. This was quite a new aspect of the problem to me, a ludicrous reversion of the situation. For four years I and all the others had been looked on and treated as dangerous to England and as potential German spies, and now suddenly we were suspected of being potential English spies and dangerous to Germany! Really this story was to continue half tragic, half absurd to the end, and this was quite a new version of the return of the long-lost sons. Reflection showed me, however, that that surprising attitude of suspicion might have been expected if one had thought of it. It must be remembered that we had not been allowed to take any paper of any description with us, so it was completely impossible to prove one's identity by passports or other documents. We might certainly be somebody quite different from the man whose name we were inscribed by, and it was an excellent opportunity for the warring governments to smuggle through a number of master spies, and they might be tempted to break this convention as others had been broken. Particularly those to go on to Germany were suspect, but those for Holland were also asked innumerable questions, and their cases were, I suppose, thoroughly investigated. This was my first experience of what made one's existence in a neutral country a burden: the spy-mania; and I gained it before I had even set foot on its soil. All foreigners were suspect of working for the cause of one of the governments at war, as no doubt many of them were, and there was an unlimited variety of possibilities about this, for did not each government employ spies of enemy nationality? If you were French you might be spying for France, but if you evidently were not, then you were probably spying for Germany instead; if you were a neutral, Spanish or Scandinavian, you were probably combining the two, and so all foreigners were suspect to all other foreigners, and to the Dutch as well, for they might be doing a little spying about the Dutch army and defences into the bargain, and in any case they were uncomfortable and unwelcome visitors for more reasons than one.

All of this, of course, I only discovered gradually; at the moment there was but the shock of this cool and unfriendly reception. But a worse shock was to follow. We were informed that a camp was being prepared for the civilians. It was not to be an internment camp in the strict sense of the word; that is to say, there would be liberty of movement outside the camp and within a certain radius. One would sleep and take one's meals in camp, that was all, and it would all be most comfortable and friendly. Only, unfortunately, that camp was not ready and one could not say for certain when it would be ready, and meanwhile we were to go to a military camp.

At that the patience of a few, amongst whom I was, gave way. Really this was too much to expect of anybody in the fourth year of the war. To be taken from a camp where after years of effort one had managed to create tolerable surroundings for oneself, to pass through the bad dream of workhouse and voyage, and then, on arrival in a neutral country, to let oneself be locked up in a soldiers' camp where one would be worse off than where one had come from. And all that to people supposed to be exchanged for reasons of health! It was too much, and we were not going to stand it. This we explained to the German representative who was a very pleasant man and quite sympathetic. Only he did not see what he could do about it as it depended on the Dutch authorities.

He promised, however, to do his best. People were leaving the ship and being entrained. One long train was going to Germany, a second to where the military camp was. The people had all taken their seats, their luggage followed them. The German attaché was still talking to the Dutch representative, a corpulent, elderly officer. I don't know what arguments he used, but certainly the Dutchman seemed to be very furious and kept shaking his head. This went on for a very long time while we, I think there were no more than five or six of us, stood, a disconsolate little group, round our piled-up luggage. Then suddenly one train moved off, and the second train followed soon after. Perhaps that was why the Dutchman gave way at last; we saw him shrug his shoulders and walk away. The German attaché approached smiling broadly and informed us that for the present we were allowed to stay in Rotterdam, after which he too departed. Incidentally, this created a precedent, and all the prisoners of later transports were allowed to stay in Rotterdam if they wished to.

Of all my experiences I remember that as the most curious. There we sat or stood near our luggage on a deserted quay in an unknown country. The authorities had frowningly departed and left us to our own devices, and we had none. For years one had been ordered about and disposed of and directed, and one had lost all initiative of one's own; now all of a sudden there was no one to tell one what to do, one was all alone and left stranded — with one's belongings — as if one had been shipwrecked. It was very alarming and very uncanny too; there was no precedent for such a situation, and what was one to do? Obviously we could not remain standing on that deserted quay, and it was equally obvious that we could not leave our luggage standing there. The only thing to do was to leave some men to guard our belongings while the others would explore the possibilities, and this we decided to do. I was one of the three explorers and we promised to be back as soon as possible and departed on our errand.

We walked along quays and across rails and through a gate which fortunately was unlocked, and on to a road. There was no town in sight, nor buildings of any sort, but there were tramrails, and after a while a tram came along. We could not tell whether it went in the right direction and we could not ask as none of us spoke Dutch, but surely it must go to some inhabited place. The conductor, after some arguments and some shaking of heads, accepted English money, which was all we had, and we were lucky, for the tram went to what I afterwards learnt was the central square of the city. At that terminus we got out and fell from grace at once, for instead of trying to find a hotel as we had promised to do, we went into a large café facing us, for we were immensely hungry. We did not want a huge meal and we did not want to stay long, but it was impossible to resist this temptation: to order food in a gorgeous café — just as if one was really a free man allowed to do such a thing!

Our imagination did not soar too high, we decided on tea, cold ham, and bread and butter for this belated breakfast, and with some difficulty and a little German and a little English we managed to make the waiter understand. Then he said something incomprehensible in Dutch and we could not think what he wanted until a man at a table close by interpreted it for us: 'He wants your bread-cards and your butter-cards and your meat-cards and your sugar-cards.' We were horrified and dumbfounded! No cards, no food; and how and when should we outcasts ever get cards! The waiter and the other people looked on us with grave suspicion. We got up and walked out, followed by stares and indignant muttering.

This was not going to be an easy task. Food we could not get; would we get lodgings? We tried one hotel which looked nice, we tried some others which looked less nice, without success. We had to explain: no passports, no luggage, interned German civilians from England — no, they did not like the look of that at all. We were extremely suspect, there was no room for us, all the hotels were full up. At last a very shady and unclean-looking small hotel, a horrible place it was, like the low-class hotels of all ports, condescended to accept us. The fat and squinting and unpleasant-looking proprietor said we could spend the night there if we paid in advance. This we did with a heavy heart, for added to all other terrors there was that of poverty. We had each been allowed to take ten pounds with us from Wakefield, but a good deal of that money had melted away during the unforeseen stay at Boston and on the ship, and God knew when one would get more, but there was no way out. We paid. One man was dispatched to fetch the others, and they and our luggage eventually arrived. Meanwhile we held council with our amiable host about the problem of food-cards. We must get them at the Town Hall he said. We went and were refused; they would not give cards to people who had no identification papers and could not show permits of sojourn in the city. They were not rude or unpleasant, but quite firm. They would do nothing for us unless we had the proper documents. There was, they said, a Commission for the interned, and we had better go and see what they would do for us there.

What a nightmare all that day was, and how I wished I had remained at Wakefield! Even the military camp would have been better perhaps, and best of all it would have been to have struck a mine on the voyage. One was hungry and tired out and weak, and everyone looked on one as a probable criminal, and one could get no food and one had next to no money, and that was how one was welcomed after all one had gone through. It was a horrible situation.

An endless tram ride took us to a brand-new building right out of the city. That was the office of the Commission. We were received by a very amiable and charming man, but he got less and less amiable and charming as we tried to explain what we had come for. He quite refused to admit that such people as we pretended to be existed; he had never heard of interned civilians, he said, there was no such thing as an exchange of civilians, there was no room for them in Holland and certainly not in Rotterdam. First of all he insisted on it that we must be soldiers, and when we had patiently explained that we were not, his face lit up and he became very amiable again. 'I understand,' he said beamingly, 'you are deserters.' But when we had to tell him we were not, he lost all interest and said curtly and crossly: 'If you are not deserters I can't do anything for you.' Apparently deserters were of much higher standing and more deserving of sympathy than we were.

There was more talk, mostly from our side, and one man had a brainwave. 'If we asked you to sign a paper just to say that we had presented ourselves here, could you not sign that?' This he agreed to do, probably in order to get rid of us at last. Such is the magic of stamped paper that this rag sufficed to get us the coveted cards! I like to think that there was goodwill as well at the Mayor's office; anyway, they expressed themselves satisfied with that document and we got our ration-cards for a week, nor was there ever any difficulty after, for, as I have already said, after our precedent the status of civilians interned in Rotterdam got legalized, internment meaning that one must not leave that city.

This accomplished, we had lunch at the hotel at last, and then I sent a wire to my mother to tell her where I was and to ask her to send money at once; it seemed miraculous that one could just walk into a post office and send off a wire. Then I went back to the hotel, lay down and slept fast till the evening. I woke with a start and when I had become fully conscious I suddenly realized that my captivity had come to an end, that I was free — after a manner; that, at any rate, there would be no more barbed wire.

Epilogue

I arrived in Holland in February 1918, and I left it in November, but when I got there I did not know how long my stay would last. In this the situation was like my previous experience, insecure and unsettled. One never knew whether it would be worthwhile to begin or try for anything, as everything might change at any moment. In that sense one was as much a prisoner as ever, at the mercy of the decisions of some authority or other. In every other way imprisonment was over, for the few restrictions did not count and were not taken too seriously. Once the situation had been legalized, the Dutch authorities left one in peace as long as one left them in peace, nor did the German ones bother at all. True they insisted on seeing my birth certificate, so apparently they were not quite reassured about my identity, and this led to a true comedy scene such as Georges Courteline might have invented. I had written and asked my mother to get me a copy of that precious document, the original of which was in England. When she obtained and sent it, it was returned to her; she was only allowed to send it through the German Consulate. So in due course the Consulate advised me that a registered letter was awaiting me, but when I went to fetch it they refused to hand it to me unless I could show them a document of identification — a birth certificate, for instance! They were quite firm about this, but in the end the Consul found a solution: on my opening the letter in his presence the certificate was revealed and I handed it to him and he handed it back to me plus the envelope, and so that matter got settled and I was officially recognized as being I.

Otherwise, however, one could forget that one was technically still a prisoner; the situation was not only modified, it was reversed. When I had been interned I had had to adapt myself to an entirely new life, and it had taken me many months to achieve the adaptation to existence behind barbed wire, indeed, I had only become definitely adapted and reconciled to it a very few weeks before it came to an abrupt end. What had followed was not, however, a return to an existence formerly familiar to me, or to anything like my pre-war life, it was something quite new and different again. I found that a new adaptation was demanded from me, that it was quite impossible to slip back to where I had stood before my internment. Not only were all outward circumstances changed, but I myself was no longer the same man. It was only after the camp had receded into remote distance that I realized how strong was its hold on me. If I had found it hard to get used to, I found it at least as hard to free myself from its influence, nor did I wish to free myself from it altogether. My new-found freedom seemed very alarming to me in many ways, and I found it as difficult to stand on my own feet again as it had been to become a number. Even the simplest actions I had to decide on seemed fraught with a terrible weight of responsibility. Camp life kills one's will, and recovering it is not an easy matter at all. I think the others felt as I did, and it was quite a time before any one of us ventured out alone. We stuck together as we had done in the first days of internment; we had not been personal friends at all, but we dared not stand alone and face the unknown, and this only changed very gradually and never entirely.

This new world was formidable, but it was not formidable in the way I had expected it to be. Naturally I had often wondered whether it would not be difficult to get used to a normal life again, and was convinced that it would not be easy. But it was not the things I had dreaded which troubled me now, but others I had never thought of at all. I had thought, for instance, that I should be most alarmed by traffic, by cars and trams and the roar of the streets. I had not crossed a street for nearly four years; I had hardly seen a car; surely that would be a terrifying experience. What I found was that it impressed me as little as if I had never left London or Paris and that I never gave it a thought. There were quite different problems to be faced instead. I found stairs a great trial, for instance, and living on an upper floor at the hotel quite terrifying after living on ground level for years. Moreover, I could not get used to staying in my room at all, since it had become second nature to rush out every ten minutes or so and walk quickly round the camp. And when I did go out, I found myself turning mechanically after a few yards — walking straight ahead was alarming — where did the road lead to, how was one to get back? — it seemed abnormal to continue in a straight line. I remember finding it extremely difficult to make up my mind to enter a shop. One only knew one shop, and now there were hundreds and how should one know which to choose? But most terrifying of all was the fact that one was surrounded by thousands and thousands of strange faces. For years now I had been used to seeing only people I knew, at least by sight; even at a distance one recognized every face. That had seemed bad enough, but now I found the other thing infinitely worse. This absolute indifference was uncanny, anything might happen to one without anybody taking the slightest notice; these people did not know one, they did not even know that one was interned. I felt as if I must stop the people I met in the street and tell them all about it: 'I have just come out of a prisoners' camp, you know.' Then they would be sympathetic or at least interested, and no longer simply ignore one as if one was invisible. It was wrong, it was inhuman that people should take no notice of each other like this! The first stranger I had talked to outside the hotel, where they knew all about one, was the barber I visited the first day, and I simply had to tell him at once. The only result was that he became distinctly frigid in manner. This hurt my feelings, but it was, I suppose, quite natural. The Dutch had only one desire, which was to keep out of the war. They did not wish to get mixed up with anyone belonging to a belligerent nation, for no good to them could come out of that. They wished to forget the war as far as possible, they did not want to hear anything anyone connected with it had to say, and they wished to see as little of either German or English prisoners as circumstances would allow.

I was still suspect, I soon realized; all foreigners were suspect, but particularly those whom war had touched. They might be all right in their own countries, they might even be heroes or martyrs or something or other admirable, but in Holland they were like people with a disease, which might be — one never knew — catching. And in all probability they were spies. That was, indeed, the *Leitmotiv* of life in Holland, and it was almost impossible to escape from it. The subjects of the belligerent nations were confined to different places: English officers and, I believe, civilian prisoners were at the Hague, German officers in Arnhem, and civilian prisoners in Rotterdam, but the innumerable people of all countries who were not prisoners could not be confined to any one place and were bound to meet. So unwritten laws came into being. People of the allied nations stayed at certain hotels, visited certain restaurants or cafés only, the Germans or Austrians adopted others. You might have thought that you would be out of the atmosphere of suspicion if you stayed in the places prescribed to you, but not at all; they were, one was told, full of spies. The Dutch who came there might be spies, and who knew if the Germans there were really German or in foreign pay? Be most careful about your correspondence, one was told, for the portier of your (German) hotel is known to be in allied pay. Don't talk above a whisper in the café; what do you know about the waiters? So it really made no difference where one went, for people were sure to think that you were either spying or being spied on, or most likely both. No doubt there were really any amount of spies about in Holland as in all neutral countries, and the Dutch, who were quite powerless to prevent this, were naturally irritated by it, but to me this was very horrible. If you went to the park there were the British convoys lying alongside it, and suspicious eyes watching you; if you went in the other direction there was the colony of Belgian refugees living on barges, and were you perhaps trying to get into contact with them? So really the best thing to do was to talk to no one and go nowhere, though perhaps if you stayed at home all day that would stamp you as a most terribly dark horse! One felt unwanted, insecure, and helpless.

But even if there had not been that spy-mania I should have found it hard to get used to this world which was so unlike the one I had just left behind, but seemed also quite unlike the pre-war world as I remembered it. From that pre-war stage I seemed to have moved away in one direction and the world in another, and so we were very far apart indeed. I discovered 'civilization' as if I had been a savage from the bush or a monk from Tibet, as if I had never seen it before, and I thought it bewildering and rather horrible. It is only long habit and thoughtlessness which make one quite satisfied with it; things are taken for granted and don't worry much unless one happens to be a social reformer, which I never have been. Now all seemed new and terribly crude. I had looked forward to a return to civilized conditions once I should have left barbed wire behind, but what I found seemed to me quite as barbaric and far more incurably so.

On the first night we went to a good restaurant and ordered a real dinner. This was what everyone was agreed on as the first thing one would wish to do as soon as one was free. It would be marvellous, one thought, not only the food and wine and real coffee and liqueurs, but the white napkins and silver and glass and waiters and well-dressed people round one. Well here we were, the dream had come true, but I felt unhappy and disgusted. After the first course and the first glass of wine I felt I wanted no more, for the stomach was no longer used to it, and then I began to think of the people in Wakefield who had not enough to eat. I thought of the millions of prisoners, the more millions of civilians who had no food and I felt I could not go on eating. It was all wrong, it was wasteful, it was inhuman to have such meals. This may seem morbid; it almost, if not quite, seems so to me now, for one just accepts such matters as millions on the verge of starvation as inevitable and knows that it would make no difference to them if one lived on bread and margarine too. But I felt very differently then. I had become used to a system where everyone got equal treatment and where there was the same amount of food for all, and I had rather despised the people who tried by hook or crook to do better than the others. So now this seemed too shockingly unjust. I had had a naïve notion of everyone living on equal rations in all countries while the war lasted, just as the prisoners were doing, but I soon discovered that rationing was a farce. Lots of articles of food were not rationed, and lots of people got far more than their share of the others; it was purely a question of money, and one could have everything one wanted if one paid enough, and lots of people were prepared to do this. The *nouveaux riches*, the profiteers, had come to flourish while time was standing still at Wakefield, and there was nothing then to restrain them. Not in Holland, at any rate, for it was, as all neutral countries, coining money out of the war. This again was but natural according to the modern ethical standard; for was there any nation or any class of people who would refuse to grow rich if they had the chance? But to my savage mind it seemed disgusting, and instead of being grateful to the Dutch for their hospitality I started loathing them. In the distance, almost every day, one heard the guns in Flanders: all Europe was torn and bleeding, and here were these people, getting ever more fat and stolid and prosperous and with but one wish: not to be reminded of the war. How very much nearer one's 'enemies' were to one, who were going through the same experiences, sharing the same fate. Surely if there was such a thing as civilization, not to mention Christianity, people would send all their surplus food and clothing and money to the sufferers somewhere, no matter where their sympathies lay. They were just hogs, I thought, but really they were perfectly ordinary human beings with a normal, everyday egoism and lack of imagination to keep them happy. They were worrying about dying babies without milk in Germany or starving prisoners in Russia or women shivering with cold in Belgium just about as much as we do when we read of starvation in China. Some people would send a contribution, most would hardly bother to read about it. Civilization is not founded on either charity or justice, and the Dutch were sending a lot of fish and butter and vegetables, the Swiss any amount of milk to all belligerents — if they could pay for them. If besides that they cared to send gifts as well, they would, but evidently there existed no such obligation. And of course they did not realize the paramount importance of food, for no one can who has enough of it. It is considered rather greedy and somewhat sordid to think and talk much about it — as long as one has plenty of it, and here there was plenty. In camp it was a predominant problem, in Germany and Austria it was, as I was to find later, the one thing which occupied all people's thoughts, but in Holland at that time it was rather tactless to allude to it, just as people who invite poor relations do not want to hear stories about their misery.

My first reaction to this was to write to the families of my different friends to urge them to send food, and to send food myself when and where I could, but I did not find this as easy as I had imagined. One could only send parcels through the Red Cross and most foodstuffs were not allowed to be exported; the people in Germany could send nothing from there, and could also only send though the Red Cross. So that is what one did, but the parcels I sent never got there. The Red Cross, no doubt, did their best, but they had no control over matters: ships might be sunk, parcels might be stolen, prisoners might have been transferred, as all those at Wakefield were to the Isle of Man sometime in 1918.

It was not only food and its distribution or — which is almost the same — wealth and its distribution which seemed all wrong to me in these first weeks, everything else seemed topsy-turvy too. I remember what a disastrous impression I received from the first place of entertainment I visited. Rotterdam is not a city of much refinement, it is a big port with a wealthy *bourgeoisie* which goes to the Hague — not many miles off — when it wishes to enjoy itself. The music halls and cabarets and dancing-saloons of Rotterdam, of which there are many, cater for primitive tastes. That again would neither surprise nor impress one under normal circumstances, but I was still labouring under the delusion that I had left barbaric surroundings to return to culture, and I had forgotten some aspects of that culture. It seemed like a madhouse. There was an orchestra of huge fat women, labelled Viennese, there were 'suggestive' French *diseuses*,[1] so-called funny men and acrobats; it was as if the world had stood still since about 1880, and there was a noisy, none-too-sober audience. No trace of art, wit, or even luxuriousness about it; it was just stupid, tedious and vulgar, and it seemed ghostly as well to me, for I had imagined that the war had killed all that. The real trouble was, of course,

---

1 French: Fortune-tellers.

that I believed the world to be more or less as the papers had represented it to be for years, for no matter how sceptical a reader one may be, one is bound to be impressed by the papers when one can't judge for oneself. I had not seen the world for years, and I thought of it as a place where everything had given way to the one great preoccupation. The men were in the army or doing war work, the women nurses, all had cast aside all other things. If there still remained any gaiety it was kept up for the soldiers on leave, otherwise all countries were places of mourning, if not without pride in their mourning and sacrifices. I had, in fact, believed that the war had changed human nature and that the world had become full of tragic nobility, so it came as a shock to discover that it had simply deteriorated all round. For the time being I thought, however, that such deterioration was limited to the neutral countries, that it was the price they had to pay for their material enrichment.

I found the peace of mind I had at last arrived at in camp absolutely shattered; I could not work, I no longer knew what to think about it all nor where I stood, and instead of writing or thinking I spent the days reading the newspapers of all nations. One could compare them here, those of both sides and the neutral ones, but that only made me all the more confused, for the two sides were in full contradiction and the neutral papers partial to one side or the other.

When I had been in Rotterdam for two months I received my mother's visit which was, of course, a great joy after so long a separation, even if the news she had to relate were mostly of a sad nature. It made me realize that some ties at least were what they always had been and that a few things could not be affected by the war. That visit was all too short, and after it Rotterdam seemed worse than ever. By now one had lost nearly all contact with one's former fellow prisoners; they also had had their relations to see them and began to feel again that there lay their real affinities;

there was no longer any feeling of belonging together, we had re-become strangers. So I was quite alone, and if that was in a way wholesome and a step towards the normal, it was at the same time rather difficult to bear in surroundings so antagonistic to me.

I made up my mind to a bold step and asked to be allowed to live in a seaside place when spring came. I hoped for Scheveningen, which has the advantage of being so near the Hague with its galleries and other interests, but that was forbidden as being in the British prisoners' zone, nor was I allowed Zandvoort, where German friends had offered to put their summer house at my disposal, but Noordwijk was at last permitted, as it had already been to a certain number of interned. So I travelled to Noordwijk, which was but a very short journey, and I was thankful when I saw the sea, the miles of sands and dunes and breathed the pure fresh air.

I have the very pleasantest recollections of Noordwijk in every way. This was exactly what I had been longing for in camp: an unlimited horizon, perfect quiet, broken only by wind and waves, and no human being near one if one had no wish for company. It was May and there were as yet hardly any visitors, nor would there be many before July, and this was a place where it was good to be alone. There was hardly anyone in the big white hotel facing the sea, which I chose, except the very pleasant family it belonged to, and when I sat on my covered balcony I had only sand, sea, and sky before me. I have always had a strong longing for the sea, and even as a child always tried to walk to it, being sure it must lie behind any hill or rising ground which hid the horizon, and no other type of scenery has ever given me any satisfaction. Why that should be, I cannot imagine, and it can certainly not be attributed to any heredity, nor does my desire go any farther than the seashore! I am a very bad sailor and don't like being on the sea at all, but besides that, it seems to shrink in an unaccountable manner once you are on it: from the shore it is immense, from a ship it looks measurable; also it is very varied in the first and very monotonous in the second case.

Noordwijk was for all these reasons an ideal place for me to be in, and it brought me definitely back to health and sanity. If I had not had that long period of rest and calm I don't think I should have managed to get over the years which were to follow it. I was there from May till far into October, but here again was a place where time stood still, as it had done at Wakefield. Altogether in a sense I now began again where I had left off there. I got books again, I began to try to re-write what I had had to leave behind. I went for long walks along the firm sands, and after a time I got bold and visited some of the Dutch towns, though that was strictly prohibited. I discovered the many beauties of Holland and grew to like the country very much. There were peaceful old cities, like Haarlem, Delft, and Leyden, and each held astonishing galleries. Leyden in particular, which was fortunately quite near and 'allowed,' has the most charming museums in the world, for the art treasures are housed in a number of beautiful old homes and not in a cold structure erected for that purpose. Visitors are few, guardians pleased to see one and ready to fetch out anything one wishes to inspect, and there are astonishing Egyptian and Chinese treasures to be seen there. I went to the Hague, which is a charming, super clean, stiff little *Residenz*, forming the strongest contrast to noisy and dirty Rotterdam (those cobbled quays!), and even as far as Amsterdam, which is surely one of the most fascinating capitals of Europe. I saw green pastures and cows and windmills and the acres of tulips and hyacinths in flower, and always there was the sea to return to.

The summer months brought many visitors, nearly all Dutch, and the hotel was full. There were quite a number of very pleasant people among them, and meeting them on this footing I found the Dutch very likable. I made some good friends, one of whom managed to arrange my Paris affairs for me to some extent, and all of whom were as helpful as they could be. For the first time for four years I felt I had re-become an individual whom people liked, or perhaps disliked, for what he was, instead of being something abstract like an enemy alien or an interned civilian. If this society was not my society of former times it was at any rate a normally composed one of which I formed a unit. There were families, mothers with children, old people, young people, babies. Some were businesspeople, some artists or on the stage, and some just human beings. They were, in fact, a very average lot, but that is just why they were the best company I could have found, for slowly and without my being aware of it at the time their good humour and common sense restored my mental equilibrium. I began to paint again, but only landscapes or rather seascapes, and they were about as simple and subdued as my pre-war work had been complicated and coloured. That summer restored my physical health and my mental equilibrium almost completely.

～

But when summer began to fade into autumn I got restless. I was feeling strong enough to wish to return to a more active mode of life, and Noordwijk was losing its charm. The war showed no sign of ending, it might well continue for another winter, for years possibly, and what was I to do meanwhile? All this was costing a good deal of money too, and I ought to try to make some, which was quite impossible there. I began to think about the future and the prospects seemed dark and uncertain enough. Visitors had departed, most hotels were closing, autumn gales made the windows rattle, and the walls seemed to shake with their fury. The seas were wild and magnificent, but it was far too stormy to be out for long, and painting out of doors had become quite impossible. Noordwijk was a sad place now, and it got worse when that strange epidemic called Spanish influenza, which swept all over Europe, made its appearance there. No air could be purer, no place cleaner or less congested, yet the disease raged and there were many deaths among the fishermen and their families, who were now the only inhabitants of the place.

The short days, nights of howling storms, the emptiness, sadness, and mournfulness depressed me terribly, and coupled with the incertitude of general and personal prospects made me feel quite suicidal and the sea inviting-looking for that purpose. Why should one go on with this any longer, and what chance was there of better times returning? In September, when autumn had begun to threaten, I had asked to be allowed to move to Amsterdam, for that was the only place which held out a possibility of finding work, or, failing that, of finding congenial company. The different friends I had made during the summer lived in Amsterdam, and I felt I should not be utterly lost there. Only the family of the hotel proprietor remained in the house now, and though they never said so and were most kind, I quite realized that they would be glad to see me go, for this was their holiday time. I did not enjoy being an unwanted guest, having been in that position now for more than four years in one way or another. I could, however, do nothing but wait and hope for the best. Though there was no imaginable reason why I should be refused permission to move to Amsterdam I had not the shadow of a right to claim it. No answer came to my letter, and I could not think where the difficulty lay. I suppose there really was none, and that the delay was purely accidental, but October was nearly over when I was informed that my demand had been granted and that I could move to Amsterdam on a certain date in November.

The great offensive of the Allies was well under way then, but I did not for a moment imagine that the end of the war could be in sight. One had heard that story far too often from both sides: if that battle was victorious or that place captured or that offensive successful — then that would mean the beginning of the end. And all it had meant was that new positions had been taken up, and everything had gone on as before. I never doubted that the war would continue through that winter, and that winter I would pass at Amsterdam.

When I arrived there the first thing that met my eyes on leaving the railway station was a newspaper poster, the most startling one I have ever seen: The Emperor of Germany had taken refuge in Holland!

I went to the hotel feeling utterly dazed. How long did I intend to stay, they asked there; how long indeed, I wondered. What was going to happen now, what did this mean to all the world and to me in particular? Even the stolid Dutch seemed quite agitated for once, and everyone was discussing the probable consequences of the event and the chances of peace. The next day brought the news that the Crown Prince too had fled to Holland, and after that all became rumour and confusion. Revolution had broken out in Germany, that much was certain, and traffic had stopped, but no one knew what was really happening. Probably Bolshevism had conquered the country, so one believed, for it was the only precedent to go by. Sailors' revolts, army soviets the telegrams spoke of, the whole of the army in Flanders and France in full retreat, they said — a disaster of immeasurable proportions. What was happening to my relatives, what would be the fate of the country, what that of people like myself? Could one return, should one return, or urge them to flight, and where did one stand meanwhile?

I paid a visit to the German Commission for the interned and found the place as good as deserted and the few military officials there quite as puzzled as myself. They had no news, they knew nothing, and the Embassy at the Hague knew less — it did not even know if it was still an embassy and if so whom it was supposed to represent! This was the end of the world as far as all these institutions and authorities were concerned, they were no longer responsible to anybody or for anything. The Dutch Commission shrugged their shoulders: surely they could not be expected to know! There was nothing for it but to wait.

I have but the haziest recollections of what happened during the following weeks. One learnt that a provisional government had been formed in Berlin consisting of Socialists of the warring factions and that an armistice was being negotiated. One read accounts of fighting in German papers, which began to appear again, and read in them tales of imaginary revolutions in other countries. The allied papers got their news from Holland or Switzerland, and there no one knew anything. The Dutch themselves got restless, there were rumours of revolution in Holland and they crystallized to this in the end: the revolution would break out in Amsterdam on the following Thursday at midday. The leader of the Dutch Communist Party would arrive at the Town Hall with his revolutionary army, hoist the red flag and declare Holland a Soviet Republic. Incredible as it may appear, this took place exactly according to schedule! At midday on Thursday the leader appeared with flag and followers and found the square guarded by troops and crowded with innumerable burghers who wanted to witness events. When he saw the troops, he declared that there was nothing doing, and left again. But the crowd was so disappointed and disgusted that something had to be done, so the Queen came over from the Hague in great haste and got the greatest reception she ever had in her life and made a speech from the balcony of the Town Hall, after which the people cheered themselves hoarse and then dispersed peacefully.

But if the situation in Holland was thus sufficiently reassuring, the news from Berlin and Vienna, where my people were, got ever more alarming and confused. I could not possibly leave my mother, an old lady, to face such a state of affairs even if her answers to my wires had been reassuring. Wires passed, but no letters, and wires too were probably censored. But how could one get there? No trains running, and how could one get across the frontier, now more strictly guarded than ever by the entire Dutch army, without a passport, without a permit? I paid another visit to that patient Dutch Commission, besieged all day by people asking unanswerable questions. There was progress to report, they said. The provisional German government had sent a representative and they were negotiating about a transport to Germany. One should have patience. After that, of course, one went to bother them every day. Armistice had been concluded long ago, and the Dutch were only too eager to send all prisoners out of the country at the very earliest date, especially the Germans, for these were now all looked on as potential Bolsheviks. That was the last form but one under which I was a suspect during the war and perhaps the most unexpected of all! But it was only natural that Holland at that moment was anxious and suspicious, between the Emperor on one side (for whose extradition and execution the Allies were clamouring), and the red menace on the other, and the deserters and the prisoners into the bargain, no wonder they cursed the whole lot of them and wished to cease all intercourse.

So I am sure it was not their fault if it was only at the end of November that I could leave the country. Having no memory for dates I have forgotten on which day this happened, yet I should remember it as the last day of my imprisonment. Once again and for the last time I reassumed the part of a parcel to be forwarded and became one of a crowd under direction. Two endlessly long trains were waiting in Amsterdam station to transport both the military and the civilian interned. I met my friend Count E. again, who had been in Holland for some time, and we got into the same carriage. We got no further than the corridor though, for the train was terribly overcrowded.

That last 'transport' showed the mismanagement and muddle apparently inseparable from everything connected with internment. The train was to go as far as a small German frontier station in the north of the country and far from any of the main lines. We left in the morning and it was about eight p.m. when the train stopped at a tiny and almost dark station. All got out, all the luggage was taken out; this was, we thought, the last of Holland. But it was not quite the last, as we soon discovered, for the Dutch had decided that there must be a *douane*[2] and that all luggage must be examined. There were two or three *douaniers* to accomplish that task, there were about two thousand prisoners, each of whom had several pieces of baggage and all that baggage was piled up in untidy masses on the dark platform. We got there at eight, we were still standing there at midnight, and they had managed to sort out and examine a few dozen pieces by that time! Then, God knows why, they suddenly decided that they had had enough. It would certainly have taken them another twenty-four hours at that rate.

We were handed over to the German escort and led across the rails to a pitch dark train. The guards wore remnants of uniforms with patches of red sown on the sleeves, their headman wore a large red sash, they called themselves red guards. I cannot say that the headman, the only one whose face I saw then, corresponded to my ideas of what a red guard would look like; he was very fat, wore a short beard and looked rather jolly. The train consisted of cattle-trucks with a few benches put in, and it took ages before men and luggage had all been stowed into it in the dark. It was, we were told, going to take us as far as Bremen.

---

2   French: Customs office.

At last it began to move and slowly it rattled and groaned along; it was pitch dark inside the carriages and outside. It seemed as if that night would never end, and though I was tired enough, having stood on my feet since the morning, I found sleep impossible. At last dawn came and in its murky light one saw empty level plains partly covered with snow. We stopped at a small station and were given the first food since Amsterdam, consisting of pea soup, which made one feel a bit less frozen. About midday the train stopped for about an hour at Oldenburg, and I had time to look at our crowd which was odd enough. There were some dozen red guards, mostly quite young men or boys, looking very ragged and emaciated; their revolutionary get-up mixed with that of the military prisoners returning, officers and men. Some of the officers were very smartly turned out and now naturally feeling extremely uncomfortable. Then there were men in civilian dress of all sorts, from breeches to morning-coats. It was an anxious and subdued crowd — being let out of prison strangely resembled being taken to it. I tried to talk with one of the red guards and to learn something about the state of affairs in Germany, but he was far too suspicious to say much. All I gathered was that 'we,' as he called it, that is, the reds, were masters of Bremen. I felt I was once more suspect, having just ceased to be a potential revolutionary in Holland, I had probably become a contra-revolutionary *bourgeois* and capitalist. I did not feel very cheerful. My friend E. who sat by me when the train moved on looked very gloomy too. He had harboured anything but friendly feelings towards the British when at Wakefield, the Dutch he had detested and declared they were without doubt the dullest boors in the world, but now he murmured to me: 'I don't think this country is going to suit me in the least,' and that remark cheered me up considerably. It was all so absurd, it was like it had been all these long years: absurd and tragic, and it was better to concentrate one's thoughts on the absurd side of things.

That twofold note was well in evidence when late in the afternoon we at last arrived at Bremen. We were officially received, by the authorities and by the Red Cross. The authorities consisted of more red guards, massed on one side of the large station vestibule. As far away from these as they could stood the members of the Red Cross, a few elderly ladies and gentlemen, mostly in black, and looking the very essence of what had now become the *ancien régime*. There was but one thing both groups had in common, they both looked grey and starved. There were two, fortunately very short, speeches of welcome; we were told by the red guards that all the luggage, except what we were carrying, would be handed out on the following morning. Then the red crowd left and the black crowd left — and there we were.

I looked at E. and he looked at me. Then I said: 'Well, I suppose this is freedom!' and he said something rather strong.

The obvious first step was to find a hotel. We went out into the station square, and the first thing I saw were some guns facing the building and more red soldiers on guard. No vehicle of any sort was in sight, nor a porter, and as the things we carried were heavy we decided to try the nearest hotel. There are a number in that square, but we found them full, as many had preceded us on that quest. So we had to take what we could get, and it came as a bad shock. No matter how much one had read or heard about the state of things in Germany, now that one saw it one was dumbfounded. Germany had always been extremely clean, orderly, well-kept, and no town more so than Hanseatic Bremen (it is, by the way, truly miraculous how thoroughly the country regained that character as soon as circumstances allowed it). The hotel was filthy, the beds covered with a kind of sacking which looked dirty and grey, most of the furniture was broken, there were various insects. It was pitiable. We had been given food-cards, and so we went out to get dinner and discovered the meaning of the word *Ersatz* ('substitute'). It was terrible, nothing was what it was called and in some cases looked like. The bread was some gritty stuff, the meat something stringy and tasteless, the coffee made of acorns, the sugar saccharine, and something served with it which looked like whipped cream tasted like lather. It was not lather, however, for the soap in the lavatory was as hard as stone and could not be made to produce any lather whatsoever. Moreover, that meal was terribly, incredibly expensive, it seemed to us. The mark had already started its downward rush, but at that time no one comprehended that fact which was to make life a misery for many years after; one did not realize that money had lost its value, one still thought goods had terribly risen in price. And if that was the food a good deal of money could procure, what could the poor people's food be like!

A short walk through the streets next morning was enough to make me see that collapse and catastrophe had been inevitable. The shop windows showed empty packages, the shoe shops wooden clogs, the streets were full of men in worn and mended or tattered uniforms, both men and women, still more the children, were thin and worn-looking, and their skin had that yellowish-grey tinge I had first seen at Wakefield. The atmosphere was one of listlessness and dumb despair. It almost made one's heart stand still to realize the immense tragedy of a great people.

The station was besieged by people anxious to get away, but no trains were running at all. Towards the afternoon I learnt that there was to be a train to Hamburg and I decided to take it as that would be bringing me nearer Berlin. It was a slow train, but as the distance is but short I got to Hamburg a few hours later. Hamburg seemed if anything worse than Bremen. The great vestibule of the Central station was crowded with people camping there, waiting for trains to run again. I was told that there might be a train to Berlin in the night. The city was dark and deserted. Hamburg had been hit particularly hard by the war, its port having lost nearly all traffic, and just then its greatest shipping magnate, Albert Ballin, head of the Hamburg-America line had committed suicide. His giving way to despair had a profoundly demoralizing influence on the population who believed themselves faced by complete ruin. It was a place of mourning, and the gaunt, half-finished new office building of the Hamburg-America seemed its fitting symbol. I dined in a deserted restaurant for some fabulous sum and went back to the station to see if the promised train would materialize.

After waiting several hours it was announced that the train would actually start, and then began the wildest stampede and rush I have ever seen. I don't know how I ever got into that train, one was literally crushed into it, and it is yet more extraordinary that my luggage was put into it and nothing was lost. Of course, the train did not start for hours, but in the end it did. We were nineteen in a compartment built for eight and perhaps it was as well that the windows were broken or one would have been stifled. All that could be removed had gone from that railway carriage: window-straps, seat-covers, even the netting of the racks. It was an awful journey, and it seemed endless, actually we took about twelve hours where normally one travels in three. Every now and again we halted for a long time and feared that the engine had broken down. It did definitely break down in a suburban station just outside Berlin, so one had to get out and leave one's luggage there. I found a tram which took me part of the way, the rest I walked.

Berlin was not as the other cities had been. They had seemed dead, Berlin was delirious. The streets were packed with half-starved looking men, there were innumerable war invalids and still more beggars, there were very many sailors — for the sailors had led the revolution and were at that time occupying the Imperial Palace. Every few minutes motor vans rattled past, full of red guards with machine guns, and skulls were painted on these vans. Intermittent street fighting was going on in different parts of the city and one heard the rattle of machine guns and sometimes the deeper sound of artillery. Endless queues of grey-looking women lined the pavements in front of all food stores; agitators were haranguing crowds in the squares. It was my return from war to peace; it seemed more like a return from peace to war, but whatever the future might hold in store, one chapter of my life had come to an end and time stood still no longer.

Afterword
by Panikos Panayi

Paul-Cohen Portheim's memoir of his experiences as an enemy alien in Britain during the Great War speaks for the tens of thousands of others who faced a similar fate during the conflict. His description of his early days in England, followed by life in the camps in Stratford, Knockaloe and Wakefield, also reflects the lives of those incarcerated not simply in Britain and its Empire and beyond but also the millions of overwhelmingly male prisoners who faced life behind barbed wire at some stage between the years 1914-19.

In fact, the vast majority of the perhaps 8.7 million people interned during the conflict[1] consisted of military prisoners captured on the battlefields of Europe and elsewhere who would spend anything from a few days to years in the variety of camps which were established. Britain acted as a key jailer because of its role as a global power in a global war — meaning that, by the

---

1 Niall Ferguson, *The Pity of War* (London, 1998), p. 369.

middle of 1919, nearly a year after the Armistice — it held more prisoners (around half a million)[2] than at any time during the conflict. This was because of the surrender of the Axis forces and because the British put the Germans and Austrians at the back of the queue when it came to returning people home at the end conflict. British troops, deployed in locations throughout the world, would be repatriated first; the enemy would have to wait.

Similarities certainly existed between the experiences of military and civilian captives as did differences. Unlike civilians, no restrictions existed against putting military prisoners to work, which meant that boredom and barbed wire disease does not appear to have affected military captives in quite the same way as for civilians. Even so, the key study of this ailment by Adolf Lukas Vischer asserted that 'very few prisoners who have been over six months in the camp are quite free from the disease.'[3] On the other hand, civilian prisoners would not have experienced the trauma suffered by those who fought on the battlefields[4] nor would they have sustained the combat injuries that proved the main cause of death for those interned in Britain.[5] However, even the combatant internees need distinguishing because, while many may have experienced conflict on the Western front, a few consisted of Zeppelin crews who survived when their ships fell to earth as well as naval and submarine crews. The latter would face, at least for a spell, worse treatment as retribution for the practice of unrestricted warfare and the sinking of merchant ships and passenger liners. Furthermore, under the Hague Convention,

---

2 Panikos Panayi, *Prisoners of Britain: German Civilian and Combatant Internees during the First World War* (Manchester, 2012), pp.44-5.

3 A. L. Vischer, *Barbed Wire Disease: A Psychological Study of the Prisoner of War* (London, 1919), p. 53.

4 Brian K. Feltman, *The Stigma of Surrender: German Prisoners, British Captors, and Manhood in the Great War and Beyond* (Chapel Hill, NC, 2014).

5 Panayi, *Prisoners of Britain*, p. 130.

officers were subject to a different code from ordinary soldiers and did not have to undertake any work.[6]

Even among the civilians we need to distinguish the different ways in which they ended up behind barbed wire, both within Britain and its Empire. While other states also incarcerated civilians,[7] Britain led the way in terms of numbers because of the amount of territory it controlled, the numbers of enemy aliens in its territories, and the strength to the Royal Navy.

British civilian internees break down into two categories. First, those on British soil when the Great War broke out in the summer of 1914, even if those affected lived within Britain and its empire for varying periods of time. Some German residents had moved to Britain or its dominions and colonies in Africa, Asia and elsewhere as part of the mass migration of Germans which had taken place during the nineteenth century. But they divided into elite migrants, including the Germans in India, and those who constituted part of occupational networks, such as bakers, many of whom resided in Britain in 1914. These individuals had established lives in the countries in which they resided and could not have imagined the changes which they would face after the outbreak of the conflict, even in the early summer of 1914. As Cohen-Portheim wrote, the idea of war 'seemed absolutely preposterous' in his cosmopolitan circle.[8] The long-term German and Austrian residents in the British imperial context therefore

---

6 For a consideration of these issues in the British context, see Panayi, Ibid. More broadly, see Matthew Stibbe, *Civilian Internment during the First World War: A European and Global History, 1914-1920* (London, 2019).

7 The classic study on France is Jean-Claude Farcy, *Les Camp de Concentration Français de la Première Guerre Mondiale (1914-1920)* (Paris, 1995). The most comprehensive account of the situation in Germany is now Ringo Müller, *'Feindliche Ausländer' im Deutschen Reich während des Ersten Weltkrieges* (Göttingen, 2021).

8 Paul Cohen-Portheim, *Time Stood Still: My Internment in England, 1914-1918*, p.20.

worked in a variety of occupations, reflecting its class system, and, in many cases, had married British women. Under the laws of the time, these women would have automatically gained the nationality of their husbands and would therefore, at least technically, have been designated enemy aliens as well.[9]

Cohen-Portheim was not a long-term resident. As he tells us, he travelled to England at the end of the 'Paris season' to 'paint in the country as had been my habit for a good many years'.[10] Similarly, Frederick Lewis Dunbar-Kalckreuth, with Scottish origins but holding a German passport, was studying English in St Leonard's on Sea at the outbreak of war but was classified as an alien enemy. Unable to return home, he spent most of the War in the internment camp in Douglas on the Isle of Man.[11] This type of experience therefore appears to reflect the lives of elite cosmopolitans, in contrast to that of longer-term residents, even though many of these also constituted elites such as those academics, missionaries and businessmen who experienced incarceration in India during the War.[12]

The geographical extent of the British Empire and the power of the Royal Navy meant that Germans, Austrians and Hungarians who strayed anywhere near British territory could find themselves incarcerated during the war. German fishermen plying their trade in the North Sea, faced capture by the Royal Navy, escort to a British port and a long spell of incarceration, often ending up in the

---

9   Zoë Denness, 'Gender and Germanophobia: The Forgotten Experiences of German Women in Britain, 1914-1919,' in Panikos Panayi, ed., *Germans as Minorities During the First World War: A Global Comparative Perspective* (Farnham, 2014), pp. 71-97.

10 Cohen-Portheim, *Time Stood Still*, p. 20.

11 Frederick Lewis Dunbar-Kalckreuth, *Die Männerinsel* (Leipzig, 1940).

12 Panikos Panayi, *The Germans in India: Elite European Migrants in the British Empire* (Manchester, 2017).

large camp in Knockaloe on the Isle of Man.[13] But the reach of the Royal Navy was global and anybody found on the high seas who crossed the path of a British vessel faced arrest and escort to a British port and a period of internment. British and German archival sources abound with narratives of such prisoners.[14] The most famous of these consists of the account by Gunther Plüschow, which, unlike Cohen-Portheim's, has remained in print almost continuously in both English and German. Plüschow tried to travel home to Germany from Kiao Chow in China via the USA but faced capture when his ship docked in Gibraltar on its way across the Atlantic. Plüschow was taken to England, where he spent time in several places of internment, including the officers' camp at Donington Hall.[15] Transatlantic passengers have left some of the most detailed accounts, especially those on the Dutch steamer *Potsdam*, which left New York for Germany with about 450 German passengers on 15 August 1914. On 24 August, the English cruiser *Diana* intercepted the *Potsdam* near Falmouth and forced it to dock. Nearly 400 of the passengers were then interned. Those considered enemy aliens by the British, German and Austrian passengers sailing anywhere in the world could face removal from ships and incarceration in countries they had never intended to visit.

British transportation and incarceration were concentrated in a series of hubs. The most important of these were in Great Britain, which not only housed Germans resident in the country at the outbreak of the conflict, but also those captured in the Atlantic and Germans seized in West Africa and transported there. In the spring of 1915, a consolidation took place, resulting in the

---

13 Panayi, *Prisoners of Britain*, pp. 55-7.

14 Stefan Manz and Panikos Panayi, *Enemies in the Empire: Civilian Internment in the British Empire during the First World War* (Oxford, 2020), pp. 100-110.

15 Gunther Plüschow, *My Escape from Donington Hall* (London, 1922).

closure of some existing camps and the opening of others. The largest of all imperial camps was Knockaloe, which held a maximum of about 23,000 people at its height, although thousands more passed through it, including Cohen-Portheim, who provided a succinct account of the realities of life here. The second hub was Canada, which housed both resident enemy aliens and others brought from the West Indies. Many Germans and Austrians also spent much of the war in South Africa, especially in the camp at Fort Napier. A fourth hub developed in India, centred in the camp in Ahmednagar, which housed not simply those living in this British territory but also others brought here from East Africa as well as Germans in Siam after that country declared war on Germany in the summer of 1917. Finally, camps in Australia and New Zealand hoovered up not just Germans and Austrians in that country but also others throughout the Pacific, from as far away as Hong Kong and Ceylon. The Holsworthy camp near Sydney acted as the key place of incarceration, the Knockaloe of the southern hemisphere, although smaller in scale.

Incarceration, including the persecution of enemy aliens, formed part of the Allies' total war against the Axis Powers. Other measures against civilians included restrictions on movement, confiscation of businesses and deportation, especially at the end of the war. These actions received support from a virulently Germanophobic public opinion in both metropolitan Britain and the White Dominions, manifesting itself in social boycotts and refusal to work with Germans, the proliferation of anti-German images, the development of organizations focused upon resisting the supposed power of Germans within Britain and its empire, the development of conspiracy theories and, most seriously, violence against Germans and their property. Anti-German attacks peaked following the sinking of the passenger liner *Lusitania* by a German submarine off the coast of Ireland on 7 May 1915 with the loss of almost 1,200 civilian lives. The ensuing riots resulted in the destruction of virtually every German-owned shop in Britain and also impacted German-owned property in South Africa.[16]

Internment therefore constituted just one way in which enemy aliens faced marginalization within Britain and its Empire during the Great War. At least 88 camps were established.[17] Some appeared in the early stages of the war and disappeared following the consolidation of 1915, resulting in the more permanent structures such as Holsworthy, Ahemdnagar, Fort Napier and Knockaloe. Camps were set up in all sorts of localities and all sorts of buildings. They often developed in facilities previously used by British troops, such as Ahmednagar or Stobs in Scotland. Others resembled military facilities, using standardised barrack style huts utilised by British troops, most famously Knockaloe and Holsworthy.[18] These two categories might represent standard types, but camps evolved in a variety of other facilities, as indicated by two other locations where Cohen-Portheim spent time. The first of these, which he passed through on his way to Knockaloe, lay in Stratford in east London on the site of an old factory, which he described as 'worse than anything I had imagined,' an impression confirmed by others who spent time here.[19] Most of Cohen-Portheim's book concentrated upon his time in Lofthouse Park, near Wakefield, the site of a disused amusement park, where he spent the majority of the war.[20] Lofthouse Park was a privilege camp for wealthier internees, who were, as Cohen-Portheim

---

16 Manz and Panayi, *Enemies in the Empire*, pp. 74-96.

17 See the list in Ibid., pp. 315-18.

18 Ibid., pp. 126-8.

19 Cohen-Portheim, *Time Stood Still*, p. 39; Panayi, *Prisoners of Britain*, p. 91.

20 Claudia Sternberg and David Stowe, eds, *Pleasure, Privilege, Privations: Lofthouse Park Near Wakefield, 1908-1922* (Leeds, 2018). Alexandra Palace, the major camp in London, also utilised an amusement park, for which see, for example, Janet Harris, *Alexandra Palace: A Hidden History* (Stroud, 2005), pp. 63-118.

cynically remarked, 'prepared to pay ten shillings a week for the privilege of being there.'[21]

The tens of thousands of civilians who faced incarceration in Britain and its Empire[22] did not form a uniform group and we can break them down in various ways. The most important characteristic lay along gender lines because, while some women may have spent time within camps, the overwhelming majority did not, especially in Britain, where only a handful, suspected of spying, were imprisoned. But in Britain women still faced the full range of restrictions aimed at enemy aliens at liberty, including early deportation.[23] In other parts of the Empire, however, some women did face incarceration, usually in family camps, because they wanted to remain with their husbands.[24] The other major characteristic which affected incarceration consisted of nationality, as we would expect. Although some Austrians and Hungarians and some Turks and other inhabitants of the Ottoman Empire became prisoners of the British, the overwhelming majority consisted of Germans.[25] Great Britain only interned those who held nationality of the Axis powers, despite a relentless public campaign to include naturalised Britons of enemy alien origin (although Australia also incarcerated this group). In religious terms, the internees reflected the German population including Protestants, Roman Catholics, and Jews, with services for both the Christian denominations in Knockaloe, for instance, while those

---

21 Cohen-Portheim, *Time Stood Still*, p. 76. The other privilege camp in Britain lay in Douglas on the Isle of Man, for which see, Panayi, *Prisoners of Britain*, pp. 95-7.

22 For more precise numbers see, Manz and Panayi, *Enemies in the Empire*, pp. 123-6.

23 Denness, 'Gender and Germanophobia,' in Panikos Panayi, ed., *Germans as Minorities*.

24 Manz and Panayi, *Enemies*, pp. 113-15.

25 Ibid., pp. 115-16.

incarcerated in Alexander Palace and Douglas could receive kosher food.[26] As we would expect, most internees were white although Cohen-Portheim mentioned 'an extremely black negro' in Knockaloe who 'knew Arabic' and 'had been arrested on board a ship.' He appears to have held British citizenship as an Egyptian, even though he thought he owed allegiance to the Sultan of Turkey.[27]

The overwhelming majority of those interned by the British in the First World War therefore consisted of white males of military age between the ages of 17 and a maximum of 55. However, the above discussion ignores a key differentiating factor amongst the internees in the form of social status. If we home in on the German community in Britain before the outbreak of the war, we find that it consisted primarily of males involved in skilled manual work, especially butchers, bakers, barbers and waiters, with some of those in the first three categories owning their businesses and therefore forming part of a lower middle-class grouping. Elites certainly also lived in Edwardian Britain, whether academics, businessmen or bankers and, slightly below them, we can also add teachers, both male and female, although these German governesses did not experience internment.[28] The parts of the British Empire which counted larger German populations, such as Australia, South Africa and Canada, would also have demonstrated a similar class structure and would therefore have counted a similar range of internees in social terms.[29] Outside these larger

---

26 Ibid., pp. 116-17.

27 Cohen-Portheim, *Time Stood Still*, p. 60.

28 Panikos Panayi, *German Immigrants in Britain during the Nineteenth Century, 1815-1914* (Oxford, 1995), pp. 110-44.

29 Gerhard Fischer, *Enemy Aliens: Internment and the Homefront Experience in Australia, 1914-1920* (St Lucia, 1989); Andrew Francis, *'To Be Truly British We Must be Anti-German': New Zealand, Enemy Aliens and the Great War Experience, 1914-1919* (Oxford, 2012); Manz and Panayi, *Enemies in the Empire*, pp. 50-73, 184-204, 250-75.

communities, however, the German diaspora tended to consist of elite migrants, especially businessmen, academics, missionaries and travellers, as the example of India demonstrates.[30]

The class issues discussed here present us with a problem when trying to fully comprehend the experience of internment during the First Word War because those who wrote about life behind barbed wire originated from these elite backgrounds, meaning that the working-class voices of the majority remained largely absent from the accounts that have survived. Cohen-Portheim, a highly educated and literate artist, needs consideration as an elite and his experiences reflect those of prisoners from a similar social background. His longing for peace and space would have reflected the wishes of those born in bourgeois households rather, for example, than the waiters who lived in cramped conditions in London or elsewhere. Those who constantly complained about their lives within camps throughout the Empire had the self-confidence to address the US and Swiss inspectors who visited the camps on behalf of the German government because they had the same social and educational status as the visitors, as revealed in the archival documentation on internment which has survived in the British and German National Archives. Internees in the Tanglin camp in Singapore, for example, complained about a variety of issues including: the very fact of internment; the unsuitability of the accommodation 'for gentlemen who have spent so many years in Tropical climate' as the 'barracks with about 50 men in each compartment are to say the least overcrowded'; and the food.[31] Even the numerous newspapers which internees published in camps throughout the world reflected the voices of educated middle class internees accustomed to certain standards

---

30   Panayi, *Germans in India*.

31   BA [Bundesarchiv, Berlin]/R901/83010, Letter to the American Consul General in charge of the interests of German subjects, Singapore, 27 March 1915.

of comfort, as such people who had the ability to run such organs and to produce the range of articles which characterised such publications, some of a high literary quality.[32]

Cohen-Portheim's narrative therefore constitutes one way in which the experience of First World War internment in the British Empire has survived. There are also the rich collections held in the British and German National Archives and elsewhere, as well as the camp newspapers. In addition, numerous other individual accounts emerged about the experience of internment, both published and unpublished. One of the few working-class narratives, by Richard Noschke, who lived in East London at the outbreak of the First World War, survives as a manuscript in the Imperial War Museum collections,[33] while the account of a leather specialist working in London have exists in the German National Archives in Freiburg.[34]

Time Stood Still became one of many German books which emerged either during or after the War to recount the experiences of incarceration by the British. One of its unique features lies in the fact that it was written in English. Published in 1931, it would have been impossible for this book to have appeared any earlier because of the level of Germanophobia which persisted in Britain even after the First World War. Few other volumes about the experience of German internment appeared in English. The first, actually a fictional account, was Hall Caine's *The Woman of Knockaloe* (1923), which centred upon the relationship between Mona Craine, the daughter

---

32 See Rainer Pöppinghege, *Im Lager Unbesiegt: Deutsche, englische und französische Kriegsgefangenen-Zeitungen im Ersten Weltkrieg* (Essen, 2006). For the literary quality of some of the articles see Jennifer Kewley Draskau, 'Relocating the Heimat: Great War Internment Literature from the Isle of Man,' *German Studies Review*, vol. 32 (2009).

33 Panikos Panayi, 'The Imperial War Museum as a Source of Information for Historians of Immigrant Minorities: The Example of Germans in Britain During the First World War,' *Immigrants and Minorities*, 6 (1987), pp. 348-52.

34 BA/MA [Militärarchiv]/MSG200/2277, Schilderungen eines Lederfachmannes.

of a local farmer, and an internee brought here from the mainland, Oskar Heine, an engineer previously employed by an English firm on the Mersey.[35] The most famous English account was a translation of Gunther Plüschow's First World War internment experiences.[36] Karl Spindler's *Das geheimnisvolle Schiff*, published in 1921 and translated into English ten years later, focused upon capture off the Irish coast, his experiences in several camps and his eventual return to Germany.[37] Similarly, one of the few other successful escapees during the War, Pál Stoffa, an Austro-Hungarian, captured in Russia and finding himself in the camps at Alexandra Palace and Knockaloe, also had his originally German narrative issued in English.[38] The German anarchist Rudolf Rocker wrote a few chapters about his experiences in an autobiographical study published in 1956 focusing upon London camps, especially Alexandra Palace.[39]

In contrast to the handful of German experiences of British internment published in English, numerous books appeared in Germany, especially during the conflict. These volumes constituted part of a propaganda campaign aimed at revealing atrocities committed by the Allies with official backing from the German government through a commission which took witness statements from Germans returning home.[40] Certainly some of the books focused upon mistreatment, including the early account on internment in the British mainland by Hans Erich Benedix,[41]

---

35 Hall Caine, *The Woman of Knockaloe: A Parable* (London, 1923).

36 Plüschow, *My Escape*.

37 Carl Spindler, *The Phantom Ship* (London, 1931).

38 Pál Stoffa, *Round the World to Freedom* (London, 1933).

39 Rudolf Rocker, *The London Years* (originally 1956; Nottingham, 2005). See also the typescript written by Rocker held in the British Library printed books section entitled 'Alexandra Park Internment Camp in the First World War.'

40 BA/R67/779, Der Reichkommisar zur Erörterung von Gewaltätigkeiten gegen deutsche Zivilipersonen in Feindesland.

41 Hans Erich Benedix, *In England interniert* (Gotha, 1916).

and the immediate post-War account by Karl von Scheidt and Fritz Meyer.[42] Both also provide useful factual information about the realities of incarceration, as does the recently translated account of imprisonment in the military camp in Skipton by Fritz Sachse and Paul Nikolaus Cossmann.[43] At the start of the Second World War, i.e., at the height of Nazism, there also appeared the account by Frederick Lewis Dunbar-Kalckreuth, with a focus on mistreatment but similar to more objective accounts and, therefore, still useful.[44]

As well as containing a strong element of Anglophobia, these, and other volumes, also spun tales of adventure, often containing stories of how the internees eventually ended up in their place of incarceration. Plüschow proves the best example. Similarly, Scheidt and Meyer and Benedix describe their capture while crossing the Atlantic and their journey to the Isle of Man. In fact, this type of adventure yarn proved popular throughout the war years with the publication of several stories by individuals captured in Africa facing transportation for the purpose of incarceration in Britain[45] and another set detailing the expulsion of the German missionaries from India.[46] Such personal accounts fed

---

42 Karl von Scheidt and Fritz Meyer, *Vier Jahre Leben und Leiden der Auslandsdeutschen in den Gefanagenenlagern Englands* (Hagen, 1919).

43 Fritz Sachse and Paul Nikolaus Cossmann, *Kriegsgefangen in Skipton: Leben und Geschichte deutscher Kriegsgefangenen in einem englischen Lager* (Munich, 1920). For the English version see Anne Buckley, ed., *German Prisoners of the Great War: Life in the Skipton Camp* (Barnsley, 2021).

44 Dunbar-Kalckreuth, *Männerinsel*.

45 See, for example, Heinrich Norden, *In englischer Gefangenschaft* (Kassel, 1915); Gotthilf Vöhringer, *Meine Erlebnisse während des Krieges in Kamerun und in englischer Kriegsgefangenschaft* (Hamburg, 1915); Philipp Hecklinger, *Tagebuchblätter über Krieg und Kriegsgefangenschaft in Kamerun und England* (Stuttgart, 1916).

46 See, for examaple: J. Maue, *In Feindes Land: Achtzehn Monate in englischer Kriegsgefangenschaft in Indien und England* (Stuttgart, 1918); Karl Foertsch, *Unter Kriegs-Wettern: Kriegserlebnisse der Gossnerschen Missionare in Indien* (Berlin, 1916); Albrecht Oepke, *Ahmednagar und Golconda: Ein Beitrag zur Erörterung*

a hungry German public during the war by combining a series of elements: adventure; injustice at lives built up over years or decades suddenly coming to an end; Anglophobia, needed to fight the enemy; and German patriotism. Anglophobia and patriotism come through in the account of Georg Wagener, the first pastor of the German Protestant community in Cape Town, who eventually found his way to Alexandra Palace and then Stratford. He wrote that 'the English always and everywhere act with bloody cruelty and unbridled ruthlessness'. On his return to Germany in June 1916: 'With a deep hail which came from the bottom of our hearts towards our Kaiser and Volk we greeted our Fatherland and roared into the German evening: "Deutschland, Deutschland über alles."'[47]

These wartime publications help to build up a picture of the mistreatment of the Germans in the British Empire and, while they may have fed a public opinion which devoured tales of adventure, the persecution of the Germans and the cruelty of the English, they usually have significant literary quality. Despite the background against which they appeared, these often moving stories help us to experience the reality of the persecution of the Germans during the First World War.

Cohen-Portheim's account, written in English and published by Duckworth, did not aim at the same type of audience. Theoretically, we might expect *Time Stood Still* to take a more reflective approach to the experiences faced, but, like many of those who wrote during the War, the book feels the same sense of injustice.

---

der Missionsprobleme des Weltkrieges (Leipzig, 1918); Otty Jessen, *Vertrieben* (Breklum, 1917); Hans Georg Probst, *Unter indischer Sonne: 19 Monate englischer Kriegsgefangenschaft in Ahmednagar* (Herborn, 1917); Therese Zehme, *Heimkehr mit der Golconda: Wie es den Kindern unserer vertriebenen indischen Missionare erging* (Leipzig, 1916).

47 Georg Wilhelm Wagener, *Meine Gefangenschaft in Südafrika und England vom 15. Sept. 1914 bis 18. Juni 1916* (Brunswick, 1917), pp. 92, 98-9.

When asked to write the Afterword for this edition, I agreed instantly, partly because I rediscovered it as a Ph.D student in the second half of the 1980s. When I wanted to approach a publisher for a reprint, I took a photocopy on my first research trip to the German National Archives in Koblenz but surrendered instead to sunny evening walks along the Rhine. While, as the leading expert on First World War incarceration in Britain and its Empire, I am fully aware of the range of literature on this subject, Cohen-Portheim's perspective has always served as the reference point for my understanding of this subject. While we cannot ignore his elite social status, his narrative brings out the key aspects of the lives of all Germans in Britain and its Empire for a variety of reasons.

First, it does not simply focus upon the years behind barbed wire but also his life immediately before and afterwards. He found himself in England painting in the summer of 1914 as he had done 'for a good many years,'[48] despite the talk of war. While he did not face internment immediately, as other Germans did, although not systematically, the outbreak of war meant that he could not return home to Paris and had to find a new place to live. He did, nevertheless, carry on working as a designer for the theatre, due to his connections, which initially helped him avoid internment.[49] Nevertheless, he could not escape the general round-up of male enemy aliens which took place from 13 May 1915 following the sinking of the *Lusitania* and the nationwide anti-German riots that followed, describing his anxiety at the announcement and the knock on the door from the policeman who told him that he should 'pack as if you were going for a holiday' (although it proved to be 'a protracted holiday' of 3 years).[50] At the end of the book, he also describes his return to Germany via temporary places of

---

48 Cohen-Portheim, *Time Stood Still*, p. 20.
49 Ibid., pp. 28-32.
50 Ibid., p. 33.

incarceration and residence in the Netherlands, eventually making it to a Berlin brought to its knees by the War.[51]

More importantly, the value of *Time Stood Still* lies in its description of incarceration, second to no other work, whether during the Great War or any other conflict, in describing that experience, even though Cohen-Portheim clearly did not face the level of privations of European Jews in the Second World War, for example. The book works especially well as a psychology of internment. It offers an alternative to another classic work on First World War incarceration, by John Davidson Ketchum, who argued that the British prisoners in the camp in Ruhleben in Berlin developed a prison camp society, involving a range of activities, because of the inherent sociability of human beings.[52] Cohen-Portheim would have none of this. He described time as 'the arch enemy' which 'really had to be *killed*'[53] and viewed the attempt to establish a University at Lofthouse Park as 'a pathetic delusion'.[54] He spent most of the war here and most his narrative focuses upon Wakefield, although he provides some insightful comments on his brief time in Stratford and Knockaloe, as well as the transit camps after his departure from Lofthouse Park. Cohen-Portheim's perspective finds reflection in the account of by the Swiss psychologist, Adolf Lukas Vischer, who spent much time visiting the camps on the Isle of Man on behalf of his Embassy and who gave this 'barbed wire disease' its name.[55] While Vischer spent much time on the symptoms of the disease, Cohen-Portheim focused upon its causes, including, in a key passage in the chapter on 'Barbed Wire Air,' the lack of privacy, in the shared barrack style

---

51 Ibid., pp. 223-44.

52 John Davidson, Ketchum, *Ruhleben: A Prison Camp Society* (Toronto, 1965).

53 Cohen-Portheim, *Time Stood Still*, p. 100.

54 Ibid., p. 102.

55 Vischer, *Barbed Wire Disease*.

accommodation, even though he lived in a 'privilege' camp, the noise, and the absence of women and children.[56] While many of the working-class internees in Knockaloe would never have known silence and privacy in their peace time lives, they certainly missed their families. The chapter on 'Men Without Women' tackles the question of sex but asserts that acts between men were 'extremely infrequent' and that he 'knew of none at all' partly because 'the camp offered no possibility of isolation.'[57]

As a narrative of First World War internment *Time Stood Still* stands as a key work because of the psychological insights which Cohen-Portheim offers, as well as the frankness with which he expresses his views, which first attracted me to the book. Even thirteen years after his release, he still feels a powerful sense of injustice at what happened to him and millions of other men (if we include military internees). *Time Stood Still* is a narrative of powerlessness and futility and therefore serves as a story of the consequences of total war upon one man, reflecting the hopeless stories of millions of people in the 'age of catastrophe',[58] the early twentieth century in Europe in particular.

I felt honoured when asked to write an 'Afterword' to *Time Stood Still*. As well as the sense of injustice which runs through it, Cohen-Portheim provides an excellent description of the realities of camp life, especially Wakefield. I hope that you have found it as rewarding, insightful and passionate as I did when I first discovered the book as a fresh-faced doctoral student.

---

56 Cohen-Portheim, *Time Stood Still*, pp. 79-85.

57 Ibid., p. 137.

58 Heinrich A. Winkler, *The Age of Catastrophe: A History of the West, 1914-1945* (London, 2015).

Paul Cohen-Portheim was an artist and writer. Born in Berlin in 1879, he lived in Vienna and Paris and was on a visit to England when war broke out in August 1914. Following his internment described in *Time Stood Still*, he lived in London and Paris and wrote numerous books, including *The Message of Asia* and *The Spirit of London*. He died in Paris in 1932.

Andrea Pitzer is the author of *One Long Night: A Global History of Concentration Camps*, *The Secret History of Vladimir Nabokov*, and *Icebound: Shipwrecked at the Edge of the World*.

Panikos Panayi is Professor of European History at DeMontfort University and author of *Prisoners of Britain: German Civilian and Combatant Internees During the First World War* and over a dozen other works of history and cultural studies.

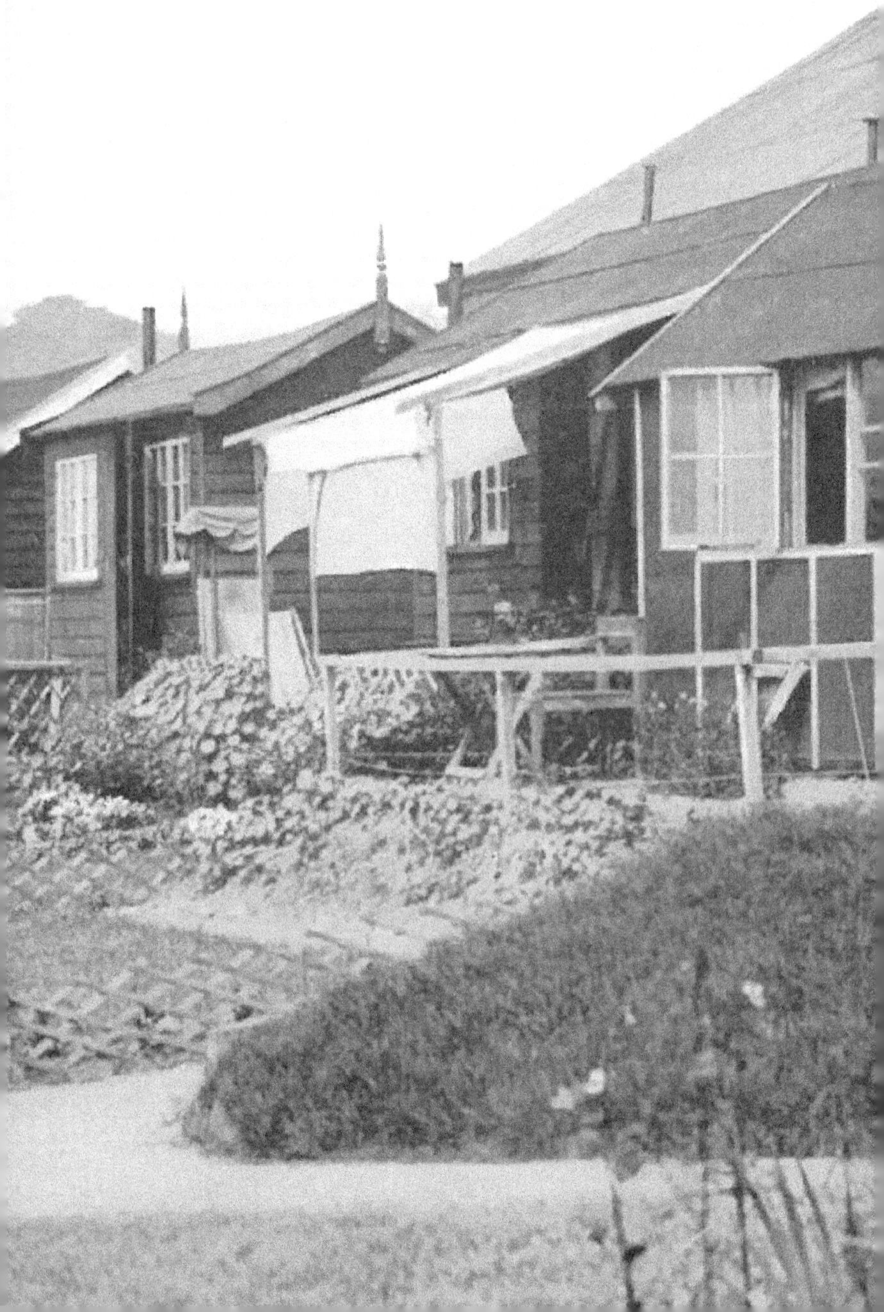

Time Stood Still: My Internment in England, 1914-1918
By Paul Cohen-Portheim

First published in this edition by Boiler House Press, 2023
Part of the UEA Publishing Project
Time Stood Still copyright © Paul Cohen Portheim, 1931
Introduction copyright © Andrea Pitzer, 2023
Afterword copyright © Panikos Panayi, 2023

Proofreading by Liliana Albertson

Photograph of Paul Cohen-Portheim from the 1931 Duckworth edition of *Time Stood Still*
End paper photographs of Lofthouse Park internment camp courtesy of Wakefield Libraries.

The right of Paul Cohen-Portheim to be identified as the Author of this work has been asserted by him in accordance with the Copyright, Design & Patents Act, 1988.

Cover Design and Typesetting by Louise Aspinall
Typeset in Arnhem Pro

This book is sold subject to the condition that it shall not, by way of trade or otherwise, be lent, resold, hired out, stored in a retrieval system, or otherwise circulated without the publisher's prior consent in any form of binding or cover other that that in which it is published and without a similar condition including this condition being imposed on the subsequent purchase.

ISBN: 978-1-915812-04-9

Milton Keynes UK
Ingram Content Group UK Ltd.
UKHW020046161123
432630UK00012B/119